The First Five Years

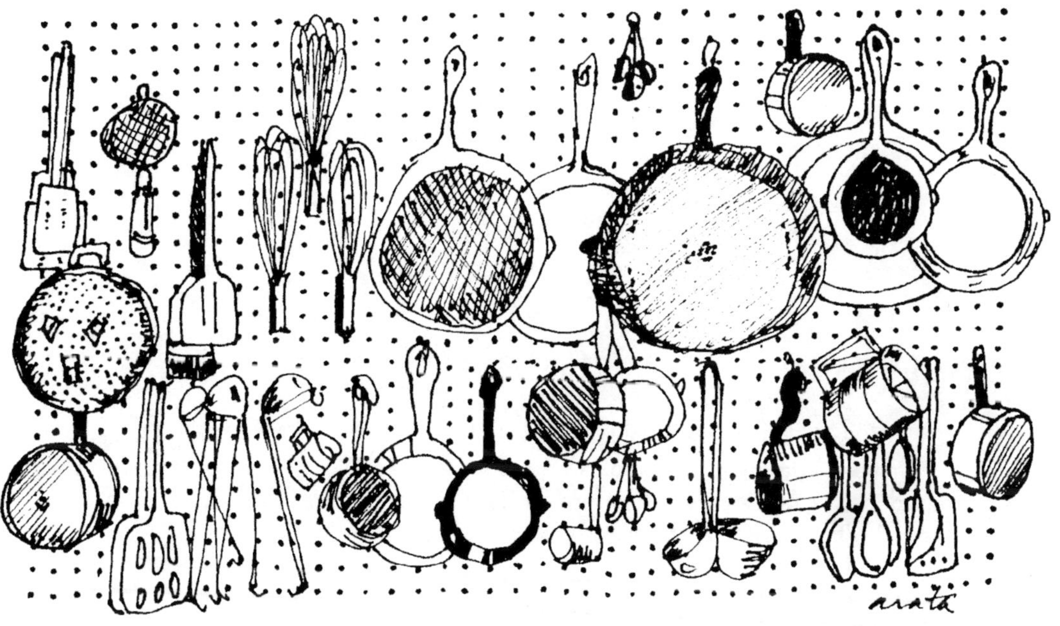

by Kyra Alex

The First Five Years

ISBN 1-57074-318-5

Printer/ Binder:
Greyden Press,
Columbus, Ohio.

Illustrations by Jayne Arata

Design and layout by Judy Shertok

Introduction

October 1991, I opened a primitive to say the least *TO GO* restaurant in the less traveled part of Oakley in Cincinnati. I had one table with four chairs and visions of quick pick ups and efficient deliveries.

From my new found customers, I kept hearing the message that my store evoked a *homey* atmosphere and made people want to linger and relax.

By Christmas of '91, I could seat 25 people, had magazines on the tables and with food and good music, encouraged people to relax and enjoy their hour or two away from the harried world. By May of '94, I had expanded into the next store front and could seat 50 people. Thus the Production Line Cafe was defined – a place filled with wonderful people from many walks of life. They allowed me to be as creative as I could be and to continually feed them fresh real foods, only to receive their continual warmth, appreciation and constructive criticism. After almost five years I find myself with wonderful memories, lots of stories and most of all, many recipes that have been requested over and over.

In this book, I have chosen the top favorites – both my customers' and mine – in seven categories: Soups, Sandwiches, Meatless Entrees, Poultry, Meat and Fish, Sides and Sauces and Desserts. I have taken the liberty of including a few of my stories and lots of tips, suggestions and findings that come from years of making fresh food, fast, and hopefully delicious.

In putting the recipes together, I found that the store really used basic recipes as a jumping off point to our creative outcomes. From a good pizza dough can come many a wonderful pizza, calzone or roll, a quick tomato sauce can spice up pasta, garnish egg and vegetable dishes or become a soup, and I've used my pie crust for everything from tarts to appetizers. Realizing this, I've given you the basics that we developed and relied on to create everything so that you can feel confident in moving from my recipes to creating your own wonderful concoctions.

Often, people will ask me how I got it to taste so good? Being very modest, I do believe everything tastes better when someone else has made it for you. This is especially true if the food has been prepared with love and care. I know that I have been given some innate talent to paint great dishes with foods, herbs and spices. Along with this, I truly care about the food I prepare and who I am going to feed it to. I find a lot of power in scenes as in the movie *Like Water for Chocolate* when Tita makes the wedding cake and her tears fall into the batter and everyone at the wedding is crying, or the love she feels as she makes the rose petal soup that consumes her guests at the banquet. Another major key is to use the freshest ingredients available and the best quality foods you can find – which doesn't mean the most expensive, just the ones that have the best taste. Cook what is in season!! It makes such a lush dish if the peaches are ripe from the tree or the tomatoes are fresh from the vine. Food at its peak is incomparable. And finally, remember that the more times you make a recipe the better you become at it. I look at the first time – especially baking – as a way to get the jitters out. Then the next time and the next I am more confident and it shows up in the food. So, respect your emotions while cooking and respect the food and who you plan to serve – even if it's yourself! Use honesty and a good recipe and your dishes can't help but taste good!!

My favorite places to shop in Cincinnati

bigg's **–** on Ridge for everyday groceries, have nice produce and good seafood and decent meats. Prices can't be beat.

Jungle Jim's **–** for that hard to find stuff. Great selection! I love their cheese aisle – sometimes you can get a great bargain on cheeses they have on special at wholesale prices.

Pipkin's **–** this place seems to be a favorite of many of my customers.

Findlay Market **–** Geieger Chicken has to be the best in the city, great meats too!!

Lunken Airport Farmers Market **–** open from May 31 to Oct 31. It is definitely my favorite place for produce. Fresh potatoes, black eye peas, tomatoes, eggplants of all kinds, garlic and much more. My favorite stands are McGlassons *(the best apple cider in the world)*, Schalk Farms and the Garlic Lady!!

Our favorite music to cook by

Vidula and I came up with this list one day – I think a lot of them are your favorites too.

Jane Siberry – great background
James – nice background
Chris Isaak – motivating
Kassav – when you need to forget where you are
Talking Heads – the job is done and you're waiting for your guests
Indigo Girls – soul searching mood
Joan Armatrading – good centering music
Everything But the Girl – great background
Aretha Franklin – always good
Nanci Griffith – want to sing along
Annie Lennox – need we say more?
Shawn Colvin – good eating music
Sarah McLachlan – good soul searching
Dave Mathews Band – great to wash dishes to
Patsy Cline – when you feel like wailing
Peter Gabriel – good background
Sounds of Blackness – when you want to change something
k.d. lang – good for anything
Tom Petty – Greatest Hits Album, a great motivator
Bonnie Raitt – if you feel like singing
Bob Marley – reggae motivation

Table of Contents

Soups 1-18

Sandwiches 19-32

Meatless Entrees 33-52

Chicken and Poultry 53-68

Meats and Fishes 69-86

Sides and Sauces 87-112

Desserts 113-134

Soups

Soups

and some basic instructions for good results with your cooking

I love making soup – you can put almost anything in it and it tastes good, even kale; and if you keep your cream to a minimum, it is almost always low in fat and high in nutrients. The soups included are some old stand-bys we served often or not often enough according to some of you. I've also included a few that were put together by sheer inspiration from things in the fridge or finds at the Farmers Market. I have tried to include a little of each style so that you can improvise with your own goodies if you want a brothy soup or a creamy soup or you don't know when to add the rice or the greens etc. If I am just playing around I usually start with the basics, onions, carrots and celery, cooked until the onion is soft. Then I'll add any other vegetables that may take a while to cook like potatoes, turnips, broccoli stems, etc. Then I'll add my stock and bring it to a boil, then add rice or beans or pasta and any greens like kale etc. and seasonings. I let it simmer until the rice is cooked, the potatoes are tender, then add the tender vegetables that will cook within 15 minutes and adjust the seasoning. I think soup is often better the next day, especially bean soups, so that the flavors can be absorbed. If you are adding pasta, try to make it small shapes like riso or orzo that won't get all soggy from the length of cooking time. If you are making a soup with just noodles and no other long cooking vegetables, then you can use whatever fun shape you want because the cooking time will probably be under 30 minutes. I never peel my potatoes for any recipe. Wash them well and leave the skin on – good flavor and vitamins.

A lot of times I want soup for dinner and it is already 5 p.m. So most of these don't take more than an hour and a half. Because of time I rarely make my own stocks. I usually buy a concentrated base – *Minors* is the best and is available in gourmet or better grocery stores. You can also used a canned broth like *College Inn*. If you are using a soup base, don't add salt until the end because many times it won't be necessary. I use chicken stock in these recipes. We would often use a vegetable stock base instead to make it totally vegetarian. Just remember that vegetable stocks are usually a little sweeter and may need some white wine or lemon or lime added to balance the sweetness.

■ I rarely cook soups with the lid on. No scientific reason although I am sure there is one. I just like to. It seems the flavors mingle better and I get a stronger broth.

■ Lime and lemon juices and wines are great flavor intensifiers and reduce your need for salt.

■ All herbs are dried unless specified.

For soups, I just throw my herbs into the pot; but many of you complained about the rosemary twigs between your teeth. You can wrap the herbs in cheesecloth and let them cook in the broth. Or, put them into a metal tea ball and let them simmer.

■ Chopped and Diced: both words mean small pieces of vegetables or whatever is specified. Cut them into bite size pieces. Picture your finished product. What size pieces of food will you want on your spoon or fork? I usually cut things between 1/4 " (diced) or 1/2" (chopped) unless I am making a stew in which I want big chunks of things.

■ Many of you asked if a soup was cream based. Only a few of mine are. I put cream in the end of some of mine just to top it off and give it a light richness and smooth flavor. You can always experiment with milk from whole to skim. Just remember, if you make a 4-5 quart pot of soup and add a 1/2 cup of cream, that is a teaspoon of cream per serving.

- When I say adjust seasoning with salt and pepper, I mean, if the soup or dish tastes flat you may need a bit of salt, or if it needs a bit more of a kick, add some pepper or cayenne or tabasco. If you want more of a specific herb flavor add more of that herb!! Make things taste right to you. Experiment. Just do a small bit at a time, you can always add more. You can't take it out. If your soup is too salty, you can try to put a peeled raw potato in to cook for 20 minutes to absorb some of the salt.
- If you scorch the bottom of a pan with a soup or sauce in it, sometimes you can save the soup or sauce by pouring it into a clean pot without disturbing the bottom of the pan where the food is scorched. This does work if the food is not too badly burned. I have saved potatoes and rice the same way.
- Large onion means one approximately 4" in diameter. Medium and small go from there. Same with a potato.
- I almost always press my garlic in my recipes. Seems to get the most flavor and is the quickest way to add it to something.

Chicken Noodle Soup

1 Tbs. canola oil
2 large carrots chopped
2 stalks celery chopped
12 cups chicken stock
2 tsp. rosemary
1 1/2 tsp. thyme
1 cup dried noodles
2 cups diced cooked chicken

Heat oil in 8 quart stock pot. Add onions, carrots and celery. Saute until tender. Add stock and herbs, bring to boil. Add noodles. Simmer until noodles are tender, about 20 minutes. Stir in chicken.

This was a soup I actually hesitated to make in the beginning of the restaurant. I had it in my head that it was too difficult. Don't ask me why! Maybe I felt I couldn't do it without making homemade stock and I didn't have the time. Finally I just did it! It turned out to be one of the easiest soups we made and everyone's favorite.

The base for this soup has allowed me to create many others just by what I choose to put in after the onions, carrots and celery. I use rosemary and thyme but if your memories of chicken soup have a different aroma, try fresh parsley and marjoram. Add a good homemade type noodle and make a meal out of it.

I would feature this as a dinner item in the summer with a dark green leafy salad and biscuits. It is very thick and as good as the corn you use.

Fresh Corn Chowder

10 ears of fresh corn, scraped from cob and divided in half
2 large onions, chopped
4 cloves garlic, crushed
4 stalks celery, diced
5 cups new red potatoes cut into 1/2" cubes
9 slices bacon
4 Tbs. unsalted butter
5 1/2 cups chicken stock
3/4 cup flour
1/4 tsp. cayenne pepper
1 Tbs. worcestershire sauce
1/2 tsp. salt or to taste
black pepper to taste
4 cups milk
tabasco

Puree half of corn in a food processor and add it to the rest. Set aside.

Melt butter and saute onions, garlic, bacon and celery until tender.

Add potatoes and stock. Bring to boil. Reduce heat and simmer 20 minutes. Add corn, simmer 10 more minutes. Combine flour, salt and peppers. Whisk milk and worcestershire sauce into flour mixture. Remove bacon from soup. Stir in milk mixture. Continue stirring until soup thickens, about 8 minutes. Add tabasco to taste and adjust salt and pepper.

Southwest Style Vegetable Chowder

This is a wonderful creamless chowder with great flavor.

1 1/2 Tbs. canola oil
2 large onions, chopped
2 stalks celery, chopped
2 carrots, chopped red pepper, chopped *(use green if red are too expensive or unavailable)*
9 cups chicken stock
6 cups diced new red potatoes
1/4 cup flour
1 Tbs. dry mustard
1 tsp. marjoram
1/4 tsp. black pepper
4 cups corn
1 cup shredded cheddar cheese
1/2 cup canned green chilies
1 tsp. tabasco sauce
salt and pepper to taste

Heat oil in soup pot. Add onions, carrots, celery and peppers. Saute until onions are soft. Add potatoes and stir for 1 minute. Stir in flour and continue stirring 1 more minute. Add stock and seasonings, bring to boil, stirring often. Reduce heat to low and simmer partially covered until potatoes are tender about 30 minutes. Remove cover and add corn, cook another 10 minutes. Turn off heat, stir in cheese and green chilies until cheese is melted. Add tabasco, salt and pepper.

I have made so many potato soups that this was a hard pick! Mostly because, God love ya, you've liked them all. But this one was requested by customers the most often of any and is also the simplest to make except the puree part, which you must do while the potatoes are piping hot or you will end up with wallpaper glue.

Potato Garlic Soup

Fill an 8 quart stock pot two thirds of the way up with roughly chopped new red potatoes. Add enough chicken stock to cover potatoes by 2". Measure this amount so that you can repeat it again the next time you make this soup.

Add 2-3 Tbs. garlic powder *(it has to be powder)*. Bring to a boil and simmer until potatoes are soft *(fork goes in easy and breaks potatoes in half)*.

Promptly process the potatoes with the liquid in a food processor – be careful – the potato mixture loves to stick to your skin and it burns! Return pureed mixture to pot. Quickly whisk in $^2/_3$ cup sour cream and enough half and half to give you a nice smooth consistency. Season with salt and pepper.

Potato Soup

with sage, sweet onions and white cheddar cheese

I included this one because it is a favorite of mine. I made it at home one day and loved it. See what you think. I had it as a meal with salad and bread.

2 large sweet onions, quartered and sliced thin
4 Tbs. unsalted butter
4 stalks celery, diced
9 cups new red potatoes, cut into small dice (1/4")
1/2 cup flour
12 cups chicken stock
1 Tbs. sage
2 tsp. thyme
salt and pepper to taste
tabasco

Melt butter in soup pot and saute onions over low heat until just soft. Add celery and continue sauteing until onions are golden and celery is tender. Add potatoes, stir in flour and continue stirring for 1 minute. Add stock, sage and thyme, bring to boil and reduce heat to medium. Cover and simmer until potatoes are tender about 30 minutes. Turn off heat and stir in cheese until melted and smooth. Season with salt, pepper and tabasco.

In the beginning, nobody would try this soup. I don't know if it was the word spicy or cauliflower, but once they did, it quickly became a favorite. It is not spicy in the sense of "burn your mouth" but spicy in the sense of flavorful.

Spicy Cauliflower

1 1/2 tsp. canola oil
1 large onion, chopped
2 cloves garlic, crushed
1 1/2 tsp. curry powder
3 medium new red potatoes, diced
6 cups chicken stock
1 tsp. thyme
1/2 tsp. nutmeg
1 1/2 tsp. dijon mustard
1 large head cauliflower, core removed and chopped into bite-size pieces
1/2 cup cream

Heat oil in soup pot, add onions, garlic and curry powder. Cover and cook over low heat until onions are golden and soft. Be careful not to brown. This takes about 15 minutes. Remove cover, add chicken stock, mustard, thyme, nutmeg and potatoes. Bring to a boil, reduce heat and add cauliflower. Cook, simmering until cauliflower and potatoes are tender about 30 minutes. Remove from heat and stir in cream.

Creamy Smoked Turkey and Wild Rice Soup

12 cups chicken stock
1 cup cream or half and half
1 cup wild rice, rinsed in cold water
8 oz. smoked turkey cut into small dice *(you can get your deli person to cut you a $^1/_4$" thick slice of smoked turkey and this should be plenty)*
1 $^1/_2$ tsp. rosemary
1 $^1/_2$ tsp. thyme
$^1/_2$ tsp. black pepper
salt to taste
1 stick unsalted butter
$^1/_2$ cup flour

In soup pot, bring stock to a boil and add rice, simmer uncovered until rice starts to open and is tender. Add cream, milk, rosemary, thyme and pepper, bring to boil. While you are waiting for the boil, make a roux – melt butter in small skillet, whisk in flour and cook bubbling, over medium heat for 1-2 minutes, whisking constantly. Remove from heat. When soup is boiling, whisk in the roux and stir constantly until the soup thickens. Turn off heat. Stir in smoked turkey and adjust seasoning.

Variations: Add corn, artichoke hearts, carrots, green beans, mushrooms or anything else you love to change the flavor.

Okay, here it is. I think Fiona and Al could have eaten this soup for lunch everyday. It is one of the only ones in which I use a roux (flour and butter thickener) but the rich taste that results can't be gotten any other way. I think that is why so many of you liked it so much!

Split Pea with Smoked Turkey

This soup definitely tastes better and has a better consistency if you make it the day before you eat it. This is my favorite pea soup and many customers who thought they didn't like pea soup requested it often.

This soup, a grilled cheese sandwich and a snowstorm – heaven!

2 medium new red potatoes, diced small
$2\frac{1}{2}$ cups green split peas
1 medium to large onion, chopped
1 Tbs. olive oil
11 cups chicken stock
1 Tbs. thyme
1 tsp. nutmeg
$\frac{1}{2}$ cup cream
4 oz. smoked turkey breast, diced into small pieces

Heat oil in soup pot, add onions and cook covered over low heat until soft, about 10 minutes. Add split peas, potatoes stock, 2 tsp. thyme, $\frac{1}{2}$ tsp. nutmeg. Bring to boil. Add smoked turkey, reduce heat and simmer with lid on until peas start to fall apart, about 1 hour. Remove lid and continue cooking for 45 minutes until soup is smooth. Stir often to prevent peas from sticking to bottom of pan and burning. Add cream and remaining thyme and nutmeg.

Black-Eyed Pea Soup

with kale and fresh corn

1 Tbs. olive oil
2 medium onions, chopped
4 stalks celery, diced
4 cloves garlic crushed
2 lbs. kale, cleaned, all stems removed and ripped in small pieces
1 large red bell pepper, diced
8 cups chicken stock
1 Tbs. lemon juice
1 1/2 tsp. oregano
1/2 tsp. crushed red pepper flakes
2 cups black-eyed peas, fresh or frozen
3/4 cup brown rice
4 cups fresh corn kernels or frozen
chopped parsley
salt and pepper to taste

Heat oil in soup pot. Add onions, celery and garlic and saute until onions are just soft. Add kale, red pepper and continue sauteing until kale is wilted. Add chicken stock, oregano, pepper flakes. Bring to boil. Add black-eyed peas, brown rice and lemon juice. Simmer partially covered for 40 minutes. Add corn, cook 10 more minutes. Adjust seasoning with salt and pepper. Garnish with parsley.

This is a Farmers Market soup. I was down there one day and was intrigued by these long purple bean pods, which I was told were fresh black-eyed peas. Well of course I bought some and after 2 hours of shelling them and turning my fingers black, I had about 4 cups of black-eyed peas. Now what? Soup of course! I had also bought kale and corn and a lovely sweet red pepper. They were destined to meet and what a fabulous result. You, of course, can use frozen peas.

This soup is so good, it was featured in an article about us a few years ago. The best thing is that you can turn it into lots of other soups. Add cooked sausage or left over lamb or pork or chicken – or leave it the way it is and eat vegetarian! It's still a meal, with salad and bread.

White Bean and Vegetable

1 lb. dried white northern beans, soaked overnight in cold water or for one hour in very hot water with the lid on
2 tsp. basil *(you can change this herb depending on what meat you add)*
1 large onion, chopped
4 carrots, chopped
4 celery, chopped
2-3 medium red potatoes, diced
15 cups chicken stock
1 15 oz. can whole tomatoes, chopped with juice

Put beans, basil onion, carrot, celery, potatoes and stock in large soup pot. Bring to boil, reduce the heat to low and cook partially covered for 1 1/2 hours or until beans are very soft. Add tomatoes and cook another hour or until soup is thickened. It will always be thicker the next day.

If you add meat in the form of a bone, add it with the beans in the beginning. If you add pieces of cooked meat, add it with the tomatoes.

Tomato Brown Rice

1 Tbs. olive oil
1 large onion, chopped
2 large carrots, chopped
2 stalks celery, chopped
1 28 oz. can whole tomatoes chopped with juice
12 cups chicken stock
$^{3}/_{4}$ cups brown rice
1 Tbs. basil
a pinch of sugar
salt and pepper to taste

Heat oil in soup pot. Add onion, carrots and celery. Saute until onion is soft. Add stock, tomatoes, basil and sugar. Bring to boil. Add rice, simmer uncovered until rice is tender, about 45 minutes. Adjust with salt and pepper.

I love using brown rice in soup. Obvious reason is that it is so good for you, but also because of the texture it retains and the flavor it imparts to the soup. White rice gets mushy and tastes like starch. Brown rice holds together and gives you a slightly nutty flavor.

Cream of broccoli was a favorite at the store forever. Then because I didn't have enough broccoli one day, I added carrots and that was it forever more. The turnips (don't gasp) give a subtle peppery flavor but if you don't have any or won't cook with them, then make the soup without them. Get in the habit of saving your broccoli stems and you can use them all up in this soup.

Creamy Broccoli and Carrot Soup

2 bunches broccoli, head and stalks or 3 bunches of stalks and 1 full head *(trim the stalks of their tough outer layer and roughly chop all)*
5 carrots, roughly chopped
1 large onion, quartered
2 small turnips cut into pieces
6 cups chicken stock or enough to cover vegetables by 1 "
1 tsp. basil
1 tsp. thyme
1 cup cream
4 cups milk
6 Tbs. butter
6 Tbs. flour
salt and pepper to taste

Fill soup pot with broccoli, carrots, onion, turnips and stock. Bring to boil. Reduce heat to simmer and cook until vegetables are tender when pierced with fork. Let cool enough to handle. In food processor puree vegetables and stock together until smooth. Return to pot. Add basil, thyme, cream and milk and bring to boil. While waiting for boil, melt butter in small skillet, whisk in flour and cook till bubbling, about one minute.

When soup boils, whisk in butter mixture and stir until soup is smooth and thickened. Remove from heat. Adjust with salt and pepper.

Mushroom Barley

This soup belongs to Vidula – my co-captain in the kitchen. She would often ask me what kind of soup to make and I'd name some flavors and we'd come up with something. This "something" was great and got written down.

1 Tbs. canola oil
1 large onion
2 carrots, diced
2 celery, diced
2 Tbs. unsalted butter
1 1/2 cups barley
12 cups chicken stock
1/2 lb. mushrooms sliced
1/4 cup sherry
1/2 cup chopped fresh parsley
1/8 tsp. crushed red pepper flakes
1 tsp. sage
salt and pepper to taste

Heat oil in soup pot. Add onions, carrots and celery, saute until soft. Add butter and melt. Add barley and saute for five minutes. Add stock, mushrooms, parsley, sherry, red pepper flakes and sage. Bring to boil. Simmer one hour until barley is tender. Adjust with salt and pepper.

I would often decorate the restaurant in the fall with gourds and pumpkins and any other goodies I could find to mark the season. I often bought beautiful pumpkins from the Farmers Market, and hated to throw them away. So, I made soup with them! I would use squash, too. You can decide what you like better. Keep in mind that you need about 8 cups of peeled pumpkin or squash to make a nice thick soup.

Pumpkin, Leek and Sausage Soup

1 large pumpkin or 8-10 cups yellow or orange fleshed squash of some sort, peeled and roughly chopped
3-4 medium red potatoes, chopped
stock to cover pumpkin and potatoes by 1"
1 tsp. thyme
1 tsp. sage
1 1b. Italian sausage
3 leeks – white and pale green part only, cut in half length wise and sliced

Boil pumpkin and potatoes in stock with thyme and sage until fork tender. Puree with liquid in batches in food processor. Return to pot.

In a skillet, saute the sausage, casing removed, chopping it up with spoon into small pieces. When just brown, add leeks and saute until the leeks are tender and the sausage is cooked through. Stir into pumpkin mixture

Add salt and pepper to taste. Can stir in $1/2$ cup of cream if richer taste is desired.

Sandwiches

Sandwiches

and many other basic recipes

Maybe it seems silly to have a specific category for sandwiches, but since I spent a good 4-5 hours a day making them for you, I thought I'd remind you of some of your favorites. Giving you the basics to the sandwiches, also lets you into a whole world of other possibilities that will hopefully allow you to create your own signature sandwiches. Make my tuna, change the bread, add avocado and sprouts or roast the pork loin, cut up some pineapple and spread on some of that peanut dipping sauce. Get the idea? Inventive sandwiches make for great party ideas and the answer to hunger at informal gatherings. Some of my best lunch specials came from peering into the refrigerator and seeing what we had on hand and building from there. If it sounds like it may be good – try it! Remember the sandwich with strawberries, brie and vidalia onion? Sounded weird, but the tartness of the strawberry and the sweet bite of the onion was awesome together.

The Veggie Burger

Makes approximately 8 burgers

7 oz. cashews, unsalted if possible
7 oz. walnuts, unsalted if possible
$^{1}/_{2}$ cup cooked brown rice *(best if still hot from pan)*
1 cup shredded cheddar cheese
1 Tbs. chili powder
$^{3}/_{4}$ tsp. basil
$^{3}/_{4}$ tsp. oregano
$^{3}/_{4}$ tsp. paprika
$^{1}/_{4}$ tsp. cayenne pepper
1 tsp. salt or to taste
$^{1}/_{2}$ tsp. black pepper or to taste

Grind nuts in food processor until you get a course powder. Don't process them long enough to make a paste. Remove nuts to a large bowl. Add cheese, herbs, and spices. Combine well. Stir in rice and mix well.

Shape mixture into patties. You should be able to get about 8 $2^{1}/_{2}$" burgers. Heat $^{1}/_{4}$" of canola oil in a skillet. Cook patties in skillet until browned on both sides. Serve in pita pocket with mayo, lettuce and fresh tomato.

This one has been asked for quite a few times, but I think I have to dedicate this recipe to Ernie at Oakley Die and Mold. My little steak and potatoes man proved that anyone can enjoy a veggie burger!

We used walnuts and cashews at the store. If you are allergic to one or don't like these particular nuts, change them – I've used pecans and hazel-nuts, almonds and macadamias. They'll give the burger a slightly different tang, but it will still be delicious. I've halved the recipe so you end up with a reasonable amount of burgers. They do freeze well so feel free to double the recipe, wrap them individually and store them in the freezer for a quick meal.

Here it is kids – my tuna salad recipe. It actually feels good to get it off my chest! If you ask anyone who worked for me, they will tell you that I was a bit of a pain about making the tuna. I may be picky about this process, but it makes a difference! Here are some key things; consistency makes all the difference. Break up the tuna with your fingers to get those big chunks out. Use a good white albacore tuna. We used Starkist or Bumble Bee. And don't just soften your onions in the skillet – brown them!

The Tuna Melt

This should make about a quart of tuna that will last a week in the fridge.

4 cans white albacore tuna packed in water, drained of all liquid
1 large onion chopped small
3 Tbs. olive oil
1/2 cup cooked and finely chopped broccoli *(head only – save the stems for soup)*
1/2 cup finely diced raw carrot
2 Tbs. balsamic vinegar
3/4-1 cup *Hellman's* Mayo
Black pepper to taste

In medium skillet, heat olive oil and add onions. Saute onions over medium high heat until soft and nicely browned around the edges. Set aside.

Break up the tuna with your fingers to a fine consistency into a mixing bowl. Add broccoli, carrots, vinegar and black pepper. Stir in onions, then add mayo to desired wetness.

To make tuna melt:

There has been discussion about what is actually better, a bagel or French bread – I'll let you decide. Whichever you use, cut it open and spread tuna on both sides. Cover each side with one slice each of jack and cheddar cheeses. Place on pan in broiler, just until cheese is nicely melted. Fresh tomato on this is wonderful!

Roasted Pork Loin

with apples, honey mustard and melted havarti cheese

First the pork loin – I think this is a fail proof way to cook the pork for great flavor and moistness. You can do this for a dinner party too and serve it with your favorite sauce or gravy.

3 lb. center cut pork loin
$^1/_4$ cup olive oil
1 $^1/_2$ Tbs. rosemary
2 Tbs. balsamic vinegar
1 Tbs. salt
2 Tbs. black pepper

Place pork loin in roasting pan fat side up. Roast in 350 degree oven for 20 minutes. While it is roasting mix together remaining ingredients. At the end of the 20 minutes, pour oil mixture over pork loin and continue to roast the meat until the internal temperature reaches 150 degrees (about 35-40 minutes). Don't overcook the pork – that's what makes it dry. Remove from oven and let sit, covered with foil for 15 minutes before slicing.

The Sandwich:

Per sandwich
4 slices pork loin, $^1/_4$" thick
4 slices granny smith apple
honey mustard
2 slices Danish havarti cheese

Cut open French bread, or any other bread of your choice, rye is great with this. Spread a bit of honey mustard on bread (we used the brand *Honeycup*). Lay pork on one side of mustard, lay apples on top of pork. Cover pork and apples with a slice of havarti and lay the other slice on other side of bread. Place on pan in broiler for about 2 minutes or until the cheese melts. The juice from the roasting pan with the pork makes a great condiment on top of the sandwich after it comes out of the oven.

People seem to crave this sandwich. Sometimes we'd be out of pesto and the look on their faces was heartbreaking. Even though we could still make a pretty good vegetable sandwich, I think the tomato pesto is the key to this creation, and many others for that matter. We made another sandwich with chicken and mozzarella cheese with the tomato pesto. We made pizzas with it, appetizers, pasta, etc. It keeps well in the fridge for at least a month and can be a life saver for unexpected entertaining.

The Veggie

Tomato Pesto:

12 oz. can tomato paste
1 cup firmly packed leaves
(you can use parsley if fresh basil is nowhere to be found)
handful of parsley
(about 1/4 cup chopped)
4 cloves garlic
1 cup parmesan cheese
2 tsp. salt
1 tsp. black pepper
1/4 cup walnuts
1 cup olive oil

Place all ingredients into bowl of food processor. Puree until smooth. Store in air tight container in refrigerator. Makes about 1 1/2 cups.

The Sandwich:

tomato pesto
5 slices cucumber
6 slices mushroom
2-3 thin slices of roasted red pepper
1 or 2 slices fresh tomato
handful sprouts
2 slices cheddar cheese
1 slice jack cheese
6" piece of French bread

Cut open French bread lengthwise. Slather both sides with tomato pesto. Layer cucumber, mushroom, red pepper and tomato on one side. Cover vegetables with cheddar cheese and other side of bread with jack cheese. Place on pan in broiler for 2 minutes or until cheese melts. Remove from oven and top with sprouts.

The Reuben

Sauce:

1 cup mayo *(Hellman's)*
1 cup ketchup
2 dill pickle spears chopped
$^1/_2$ tsp. salt
$^1/_2$ tsp. cayenne pepper

Mix all ingredients until well combined. Makes about 2 cups.

The Sandwich:

2 pieces of rye bread
3-4 oz. thinly sliced corned beef
2 Tbs. sauerkraut
2 slices Swiss cheese
reuben sauce

Spread a nice amount of sauce on both sides of bread. Stack meat, then sauerkraut and then cheese on one side of bread. Place both sides open face on pan into broiler and broil until cheese is melted.

A lot of people said we had a really good reuben. Since we didn't do anything special for the corned beef, I can only assume it was the sauce that makes it so good, and the love, of course, that goes into making them!

When I was a kid, tartar sauce was the only way you'd get me to eat those fish sticks everybody's mother seemed to love, that, and the macaroni and cheese that would often accompany the meal. Well, the first time Lent rolled around, my good Catholic employees pointed out that I had a bit of a responsibility at lunch time to serve fish. I took on the challenge (mostly to create a good fish sandwich) and soon we had a reputation for a great fish sandwich. Everyone said the fish was great, but I still think it's the tartar sauce!

Crispy Oven Baked Fish Sandwich

Oven Baked Fish:

$2^1/_2$ lbs. mild white fish fillets
(I used fresh ocean perch)
1 cup of milk
2 cups of fine bread crumbs
$^1/_4$ cup grated parmesan cheese
$^1/_2$ tsp. thyme
$^1/_2$ tsp. oregano
$^1/_2$ tsp. basil
$^1/_2$ tsp. paprika
$^1/_4$ tsp. cayenne pepper
salt to taste
4 Tbs. melted butter

Rinse off fish and check for bones. Pour milk into bowl big enough to dip fish fillets. Mix bread crumbs with cheese herbs and spices and place in another bowl big enough to dip fish fillets. Take each fillet, dip it in milk and then dredge in bread crumbs, shaking off excess. Place on baking tray. Drizzle with melted butter.

Bake in 400 degree oven for 15-20 minutes or until lightly browned and flaky when tested with a knife.

Serve on bread with tartar sauce, lettuce, tomato, etc.

Tartar Sauce:

2 cups mayo (Hellman's)
2 dill pickle spears chopped
1 Tbs. horseradish
$^3/_4$ tsp. sugar
$^1/_2$ tsp. dill
$^1/_2$ tsp. salt
squeeze of lemon juice
$^1/_2$ tsp. paprika
$^1/_4$ tsp. cayenne

Combine ingredients and mix well. Makes about 2 cups.

Salami, Melted Mozzarella & Artichoke Sandwich

with house vinaigrette

Ahhh, my house vinaigrette! I live with a person who drinks this vinaigrette from a jar, so needless to say, I take dressings very seriously.

A good vinaigrette can jazz up anything, sandwiches, meats, greens and pasta salads. This recipe includes a good basic Italian dressing that keeps in the refrigerator in a jar for months. This sandwich is decadent and dedicated to the Ackmor boys.

Vinaigrette:

$1/2$ cup red wine vinegar
2 cloves garlic
2 Tbs. parmesan cheese
1 tsp. oregano
$1\,1/2$ tsp. basil
black pepper to taste
1 Tbs. dijon mustard
1 tsp. sugar
dash salt
$1/2$ cup olive oil
$1/2$ canola oil

Put all ingredients except oils in bowl of food processor and process for 6 seconds to combine. With motor running, add olive oil first in a steady stream, and then the canola oil. Process until well combined. Makes about $1\,1/2$ cups.

Sandwich:

10 thin slices salami (about $1/8$ of a lb.)
1-2 canned artichoke hearts sliced thin
2-3 slices mozzarella cheese
handful of watercress cleaned and trimmed of $1/2$" of stem from bottom
6 " piece of French bread

Cut open French bread lengthwise and cover with mozzarella cheese. Place in broiler open face to melt cheese about 2 minutes. Remove bread and lay salami over one side, top with artichoke hearts and watercress. Drizzle about 1 Tbs. vinaigrette over sandwich and serve warm.

The first time I made these, the consistency was terrible! I had used canned garbanzo beans which resulted in a mushy, oil soaked patty. Then I did some research and found that I shouldn't use cooked beans, just dried beans, that had been soaked overnight in cold water to soften them. Well, this was the key and even though I had a hard time getting people to try them again, they did finally prevail!

Falafel

Serves 4

1 cup dry garbanzo beans or chick peas, soaked overnight in cold water
4 cloves garlic
1 cup tightly packed cilantro stems and leaves both *(a lot of the flavor of fresh cilantro is in the stems so don't just use the leaves)*
$^1/_4$ cup olive oil
1 Tbs. + 1 tsp. cumin
$^1/_2$ tsp. turmeric
$^1/_2$ tsp. oregano
1 $^1/_8$ tsp. salt
$^1/_4$ tsp. cayenne
squeeze of fresh lemon juice if you have it

Drain beans and place in bowl of food processor. Add cilantro, garlic and olive oil and process until smooth, scraping the sides down to get it all. Remove to mixing bowl. Add remaining ingredients and stir to blend.

Shape into 2" patties about $^1/_2$" thick. Heat $^1/_2$" oil in large skillet and pan fry falafel until nicely browned on both sides. Makes about 12 patties and can easily be doubled.

Cucumber Yogurt Sauce:

1$^1/_2$ cups plain yogurt
1 cup chopped cucumber
2 Tbs. chopped fresh mint
$^3/_4$ tsp. salt or to taste
fresh cracked black pepper to taste

Stir ingredients together to a nice smooth consistency with chunks of cucumber.

Grilled Mediterranean Sandwich

I stopped making these at the store when we started getting really busy at lunch because I didn't have the personpower to grill each sandwich. But these are so good and could even work as an appetizer if you cut the sandwiches into bite-size pieces.

Makes 4-6 sandwiches

1 lb. bag fresh spinach leaves, rinsed and stemmed
1 Tbs. butter
1 cup grated mozzarella cheese
5 ounces crumbled feta cheese *(we used Israeli sheep's milk feta)*
$^{1}/_{2}$ cup chopped red onion
1 Tbs. fresh lemon juice
salt and pepper to taste

Melt butter in skillet, add spinach leaves and saute until wilted and all liquid evaporates, about 5 minutes. Remove to bowl, add mozzarella, feta, onion, lemon juice and salt and pepper to taste. Mix thoroughly.

To make sandwiches:

Butter 1 side of 2 pieces of whole grain bread, place about a $^{1}/_{2}$ cup of spinach mixture on unbuttered side of one slice of bread, cover with other slice, butter side up. Heat a skillet and place buttered side down in pan, browning evenly, about 2-4 minutes, flip and brown other side. Serve warm.

I have made so many chicken salads, some I really like and some I didn't, but for a sandwich I always come back to my original recipe. Basic, simple and comforting. And, thanks to those Milacron men who would walk that bridge to get to this stuff.

Chicken Salad Sandwich

Serves 4

2 whole boneless breasts of chicken, about 1 lb.
1 granny smith apple, peeled, cored and chopped into small pieces
2-3 stalks celery, diced
salt and pepper to taste
$^1/_2$-$^3/_4$ cup mayo *(Hellman's)*

Oven *poach* chicken by placing the breasts in a low sided pan and adding $^1/_4$" of water or white wine. Drizzle with olive oil and sprinkle with salt and pepper. Bake in 350 degree oven 25 minutes or until just cooked through. Do not overcook the meat. Remove and let cool.

Cut chicken into small ($^1/_2$" pieces) and place in mixing bowl with apples, celery, salt and pepper. Toss to combine, then stir in mayonnaise to desired wetness.

Serve on wheat bread with lettuce or watercress and tomato, etc.

Egg Salad with Capers on Rye

with cucumbers and watercress and melted havarti

Makes about 4 sandwiches

Egg salad:

The key here is – don't overcook your eggs! They get green and rubbery.

Place 6 eggs in a saucepan just big enough to hold them. Cover with cold water and place over medium-high heat to boil. As soon as water begins to boil, set timer to cook eggs for 8 minutes. Promptly remove eggs and run under cold water for a few minutes to stop the cooking process. When eggs are cool to touch, peel and chop into a mixing bowl. I like to chop it pretty fine so there aren't any big white pieces.

Add to eggs:

1 tsp. horseradish
2 Tbs. capers, drained
salt and pepper to taste

Toss to combine and then stir in approximately 3 Tbs. of mayonnaise (*Hellman's*) until moist.

Place a slice of havarti on each of 2 slices of rye bread and melt in broiler. Remove and add egg salad, slices of cucumber and watercress, and tomato if in season.

Ham or Canadian bacon is also good and makes a great brunch sandwich.

Everybody asked for egg salad when I didn't have any and when I made it, nobody asked for it. So, I started running it as a special, and it became quite popular. Of course, everyone wanted to know what those green things were that tasted so good in there! They are capers and you can find them in the olive section of your grocery store.

This egg salad also makes a great spread for crackers. When I was little, my mom also served egg salad with capers on top in a little bowl at her cocktail parties – I guess that's where I got this idea.

When tomatoes are in season they make an excellent addition to this sandwich.

Meatless Entrees

Meatless Entrees

When I opened the restaurant, I didn't consciously plan on having so many meatless choices, but over time I realized that they were favorites of both mine and a lot of my customers. I can't say I am a *vegetarian* – I love turkey and sneak salami sandwiches every so often and my favorite thing to order in a restaurant is a well prepared pork loin. But on an everyday basis, I enjoy cooking with beans, vegetables, rice and potatoes. I have even managed to make kale taste good and feel so good when eating it. I don't think these dishes are compromises to a good steak dinner. In fact, I feel they are wonderful alternatives to the meat and starch grind.

Shepherd's Pie

I put this together years ago on a snowy evening because I wanted "healthy" comfort food. It hit the mark for me and also became one of the most asked for recipes by my customers.

Serves 6-8

Filling

1 1/2 cups green lentils
1 Tbs. olive oil
1 large onion cut in half and sliced thin
1 28 oz. can whole tomatoes with juice, chopped
1 1/2 Tbs. soy sauce or tamari
1/2 cup chopped parsley
1/2 tsp. basil
1 tsp. fines herbes *(an herb mix, should be in the better spice section at the store)*
salt and pepper to taste

Place lentils in sauce pan and cover by 3" of cold water. Bring to boil and simmer until lentils are tender but still holding shape. Drain. In a large skillet heat olive oil. Add onions and saute over medium heat until soft and golden brown. Remove from heat. Place lentils in large mixing bowl, add onions and remaining ingredients. Toss to combine well. Place in greased 9x13" baking pan.

Mashed potatoes for top:

3 medium new red potatoes *(about 3" diameter)*
3 1/2 Tbs. salted butter
1/4 cup + 2 Tbs. milk
3/4-1 tsp. salt or to taste
black pepper to taste
dash granulated garlic optional

Completely cover potatoes with cold water by 1". Bring to boil and simmer until potatoes are tender and fall apart when fork is inserted. Don't overcook your potatoes – they will have a mushy watery consistency if you let them cook too long. Drain and immediately add butter, milk, salt and pepper and garlic if you choose. Whip with electric beaters or hand masher until smooth. Add more milk if too stiff. Spoon potatoes onto lentils and spread evenly to cover top. Bake in preheated 350 degree oven for 45 minutes or until top is golden and lentil mixture is bubbling.

Spanakopita

I have had many a spinach pie wrapped in filo dough and I have to agree with my customers – these are delicious. They really aren't that hard to make. The filling is a snap. Get good feta cheese. We used Israeli sheep's milk feta, its creamy and mild. The filo dough does take patience but if you keep it covered as you use it so it doesn't dry out, you won't have too much trouble. If it rips while you're working with it, just piece it together. By the time it comes out of the oven no one will know the difference. We made individual triangle shaped pies at the store. You can do this if you want to make small ones for appetizers. For the purpose of making this an easy meal, I've given you instructions on how to layer it in a 9x13" pan.

Serves 6

1 Tbs. olive oil
1 medium onion, chopped
2 cloves garlic, crushed
1 16 oz. bag frozen leaf spinach thawed and all the liquid squeezed out of it
1 Tbs. lemon juice
1 tsp. oregano
$^1/_2$ tsp. dill
pepper to taste *(I go a little heavy on the pepper)*
1 lb. feta cheese, crumbled
salt to taste
16 sheets of filo dough
2 sticks unsalted butter, melted

Heat oil in skillet and add onions and garlic. Saute until onions are soft and translucent. Add spinach, lemon juice, oregano, dill and pepper, saute until heated through, about 5 minutes. Remove from heat and stir in feta and salt to taste.

Lay out filo sheets on work table. Brush a sheet with melted butter and place inside greased 9x13" baking pan. Do this to 7 more sheets stacking them on top of each other in pan, letting sides overhang. Place spinach mixture in pan and spread evenly over buttered sheets. Cover with last 8 sheets, buttered and roll edges up into pan to form a decorative edge.

Score pie into 12 wedges, being careful to only cut half way through.

Bake in 400 degree oven for approximately 25 minutes or until filo is bronzed and flaky.

Mashed Potato Leek Pie

Serves 4-5

1 10" pie crust *(see index for recipe)*
2 cups mashed potatoes, preferably cold
1 lb. cottage cheese
2 eggs
1/2 cup sour cream
1 1/2 tsp. salt
1/4 tsp. cayenne pepper
3 Tbs. butter
2 leeks, white and pale green part only, cut lengthwise and sliced
2 Tbs. grated parmesan cheese

Melt butter in medium skillet, add leeks and saute until tender. Remove from heat.

Roll out pie crust to fit 9-10" pie plate and trim and crimp edges for a decorative border.

Place cottage cheese and eggs in bowl of food processor and puree until nice and smooth. Place in mixing bowl. Add potatoes, sour cream, salt, and cayenne pepper, whisk until fairly smooth, stir in leeks.

Pour mixture into pie crust and smooth top. Sprinkle parmesan cheese over pie.

Bake in 350 degree oven for 45-50 minutes until pie is golden and just set in the center. Remove from oven and let sit for at least 15 minutes before cutting.

This is a great way to use up leftover mashed potatoes or a good reason to make too many mashed potatoes in the first place!! A lot of my customers have tried to recreate this pie at home and have had good results. Here is the original version. This is probably my most favorite dish in this book and makes a great brunch, lunch or light supper.

To clean leeks:

Cut them first and then run them under cold water in a colander – best way to remove all the grit.

I love shitake mushrooms and fresh sage. I love, even more, cheese ravioli. So this is one of my favorite pasta dishes. It is simple, quick and with a nice salad and good bread makes an elegant dinner.

Vidula successfully made this lower in fat by using condensed skim milk instead of cream.

Cheese Ravioli
with shitake mushrooms and fresh sage

Serves 4-5

1 lb. cheese ravioli *(cooked according to directions, drained and tossed in olive oil to prevent sticking)*
$1\frac{1}{2}$ tsp. olive oil
4 green onions, sliced
1 clove garlic, crushed
4 oz. shitake mushrooms, sliced
1 cup chicken stock
$\frac{1}{4}$ cup chopped fresh sage *(you can use 1 Tbs. dried if fresh is unavailable)*
1 cup light cream
salt and pepper to taste
freshly grated parmesan cheese
chopped flat leaf parsley for garnish

Heat olive oil in large skillet. Add green onions and garlic and saute for 1 minute, add shitake mushrooms and saute another 3 minutes until just soft. Add stock and sage and bring to boil. Simmer for 10 minutes.

Add cream and simmer another 8 minutes or until desired sauce consistency. I like my pasta sauces a little runny so the starch from the pasta doesn't dry the dish out. Serve over ravioli with parmesan and parsley.

Basil, Tomato and Feta Cheese Quiche

When Mrs. Schick asked me to make her a few quiches for a brunch, she mentioned tomatoes and basil and left the rest up to me. I wanted something simple but elegant. She was very pleased with the results and I think this makes a fabulous summer dinner fare or wonderful brunch/lunch gathering entrée.

Serves 6-8

5-6 roma tomatoes, diced
1/2 cup fresh basil, shredded
6 oz. feta cheese, crumbled
6 eggs
1 cup cream
salt and pepper to taste
1 10" pie crust *(see index for recipe)*

Roll out crust to hang over a 9-10" pie pan by 1". Trim and roll edge to make decorative border around plate. Cover bottom of crust with tomatoes, then the feta cheese and then the basil.

Whisk eggs until light and frothy, whisk in cream and salt and pepper to taste. Pour over tomato mixture in crust.

Bake at 350 degrees for 35-40 minutes or until just set in middle.

Remove from oven and allow to cool 15 minutes before cutting.

It was 4 o'clock and I hadn't even started the dinner for the evening pick up. The menu said Handmade Pizza with greens, garlic and mushrooms.

This is what they got and boy did it look good. Francis, one of my cooks, recreated it at home and said it was wonderful. So I decided to include it here. With this recipe you get a good, fast pizza dough recipe that can be used for pizzas, calzones and simple dinner rolls. Also how to roast garlic – a wonderful condiment to have on hand for breads, whipped into mashed potatoes, tossed with pasta, in soup, whatever!

Pizza

with roasted garlic, spinach and mushrooms

Serves 4

To roast garlic:

Slice off tops of 3 whole heads of garlic, unpeeled, exposing the tops of each clove. Place sliced top up in roasting pan, drizzle with olive oil and bake in 375 degree oven for about 35-40 minutes or until very soft. Squeeze the meat out of the skin and mash it into a soft spread.

For pizza dough:

3 1/2 cups unbleached white flour
1 package rapid rise yeast
3/4 tsp. salt
1 1/4 cups warm water (110 degrees)
1 Tbs. olive oil
2 tsp. honey

Place 2 1/2 cups flour in large mixing bowl with yeast and salt, toss to combine. Stir together water, oil and honey and add to flour. Beat with spoon until dough is smooth, about 5 minutes. Stir in 1/2 cup of flour and turn out onto counter. Knead dough adding up to 1/2 cup more flour until smooth and elastic. Place in oiled bowl and cover with cloth. Let rise in warm place *(I put mine on top of the preheated stove)* for 20 minutes or until doubled. Punch down and turn onto table covering with inverted bowl. Let rest 10 minutes. Roll out and shape to fit pizza pan. Will fit one 11x17 " pan or two 12" round pans.

Remaining toppings:

1 Tbs. olive oil
3/4 lb. mushrooms sliced
1/2 tsp. thyme
1 red onion, roughly chopped
1 lb. fresh spinach, stemmed
1/2 tsp. oregano
salt and pepper to taste
1 lb. mozzarella cheese, shredded

Heat olive oil in large skillet, saute mushrooms with thyme until just starting to soften, add onion and continue cooking until all liquid evaporates. Add spinach, oregano and salt and pepper to taste. Saute until spinach is wilted and tender. Remove from heat.

Smear dough in pan with roasted garlic spread, drizzle with olive oil and sprinkle with salt and pepper lightly. Distribute spinach mixture evenly over crust and top with shredded cheese.

Bake in 400 degree oven for 15-20 minutes or until cheese is melted, golden and bubbly and crust edges are nicely browned.

Other pizza ideas:

Artichoke pate *(see index for recipe)*
grilled vegetables
cheddar cheese

Tomato pesto *(see index for recipe)*
grilled eggplant
mozzarella cheese

Tomato sauce *(see index for recipe)*
mushrooms
Greek olives
havarti cheese

I didn't understand polenta very well in the beginning. Then, I read somewhere to think of it as a base, like pasta and top it likewise. That was all I needed – I was off! I prefer to bake my polenta, making it firm. This recipe has three components to it that can all be used as a catalyst for many other recipes using one, or all . Together, they can't be beat.

Polenta

with sauteed spinach, grilled portabella mushrooms and tomato sauce

Serves 6-8

Polenta:

This is Vidula's version and we thought it was great!

$1\frac{1}{2}$ cups boiling water
1 tsp. salt
1 cup cold water
1 cup cornmeal
$\frac{1}{2}$ cup grated parmesan cheese
2 Tbs. unsalted butter

Whisk cornmeal into cold water and add this to boiling water with salt. Stir constantly over medium heat until mixture resembles runny mashed potatoes. Remove from heat and stir in parmesan cheese and butter. Pour onto greased cookie sheet. Bake in 350 degree oven for 20 minutes or until golden and just firm to touch.

Mushrooms:

8-10 stemmed portabello mushrooms
$\frac{1}{2}$ cup my vinaigrette *(see index for recipe)*

Place mushrooms stem side up on plate and pour a bit of vinaigrette into each one. Let marinate for 2 hours.

Grill over hot coals, 5 minutes per side.

Tomato Sauce:

1 Tbs. olive oil
1 large onion, chopped
2 cloves garlic, crushed
6 cups chopped tomatoes, canned or fresh
1 1/2 tsp. basil
dash sugar
salt and pepper to taste

Heat oil in skillet, add onion and garlic, saute until soft. Add tomatoes, basil, sugar and salt and pepper. Simmer until thickened and flavors have mingled, about 25 minutes.

Spinach:

2 lbs. fresh spinach stemmed and ripped into small pieces
2 Tbs. olive oil
3 cloves garlic, crushed

Heat oil in large skillet, add spinach and toss to coat with oil, saute until wilted and tender.

To assemble:

Cut polenta into 2" squares. Top with tomato sauce, spinach and then julienned mushrooms. Serve with crumbled feta or goat cheese.

This has got to be the healthiest dish I make! And, it tastes good!! The real trick with kale is to be thoughtful with it. Remove all the tough stems, even up into the leaf part, and rip it up, don't cut it with a knife. I read somewhere that cutting kale changes its texture. This recipe is for Mrs. Stegman, whose eyes rolled around when she told me how much she liked this dinner.

Sauteed Kale

with sweet red peppers and onions

Serves 4-5

2 cups cooked brown rice *(Bring 4 cups of water to a boil with 1 Tbs. butter in it. Add rice and stir, bring back to boil, cover and reduce heat to low and cook undisturbed for 45 minutes, or until water is absorbed. Fluff with a fork. If you like soft rice, cook it with a little extra water and let it sit with the lid on after it is finished. If you like firmer rice, remove the lid as soon as it is done cooking and let it stand.)*

2 Tbs. olive oil
3 small onions, quartered and sliced thick
1 large sweet red bell pepper, cut into 1" pieces
2 lbs. kale, washed well, all stems removed and ripped into bite size pieces
4 cups chicken stock
1 1/2 tsp. oregano
1/3 cup white wine
1/4 tsp. crushed red pepper flakes
salt and pepper to taste

In the largest skillet you have, heat the olive oil, add onions and over medium high heat saute them until browning around edges. Add red pepper and cook another 3 minutes. Add kale, tossing it so it is coated with pan oil and wilted. You will have to do this in bunches, but don't get discouraged, it will all fit. It takes a few minutes for each bunch to cook down enough to fit more in. And yes, you will drop some on the floor and on the stove. Vidula became extremely annoyed with this. The whole process takes about 10-15 minutes. When all your kale is in, add the oregano and red pepper flakes, combine well, stir in stock and white wine and bring to boil. Reduce heat to a gentle simmer and cook uncovered until liquid is evaporated. Takes about 45 minutes. Serve over rice with freshly grated parmesan cheese.

Black Bean Lasagna

It is really simple to put this dish together and is a great change from traditional lasagna. Thanks to Jim and Pat, we discovered that canned beans make a runnier lasagna and I suggest you take the time to cook off your own beans. If you do use canned beans, drain them well.

Serves 6-8

12-15 cooked lasagna noodles
$1\frac{1}{2}$ cups sour cream
1 lb. cheddar cheese, shredded
$1\frac{1}{2}$-2 cups dried black beans, soaked and then cooked in boiling water until soft, about $1\frac{1}{2}$ hours *(You can soak them overnight in cold water or you can soak them for an hour covered in very hot water. Always drain your soaking water and cook beans in fresh cold water to cover.)*
salsa sauce – recipe to follow

Salsa Sauce:

1 28 oz. can crushed tomatoes
3 15 oz. cans whole tomatoes with juice, chopped
1 bunch cilantro, chopped *(use stems too)*
4 cloves garlic, crushed
1 4 oz. can green chilies
2 Tbs. olive oil
$\frac{1}{4}$ cup red wine vinegar
1 Tbs. cumin
1 tsp. tabasco or to taste
salt and pepper to taste

Combine all ingredients until mixed well.

To assemble:

Place a $\frac{1}{2}$ cup of salsa on bottom of 9x13" baking pan. Cover pan with one layer of noodles. Spread noodles with 2 cups sauce. Dollop half of sour cream evenly over sauce and spread slightly. Pour half of black beans over sour cream, sprinkle lightly with salt. Cover beans with half of cheddar cheese. Repeat this procedure one more time starting with noodles. End with a layer of noodles and cover with remaining sauce.

Bake at 350 degrees for 45 minutes to 1 hour until bubbly and heated through.

This recipe is about three different recipes combined so that I could end up with all my favorites in one dish. Use this recipe as a catalyst and put whatever vegetables or cheeses you want in it. I use Navy beans because I like my beans small and a bit more subtle. You can change this if you'd like or add others like fava beans or black eyed peas- have fun!

White Bean and Vegetable Gratin

with goat or feta cheese

Serves 6

2 Tbs. olive oil
1 cup dried small white navy beans, soaked in cold water overnight or hot water for an hour, covered
1 bay leaf
1 tsp. salt
3 leeks, white and pale green part only, sliced
1 can artichoke hearts, drained and quartered
1 bag frozen leaf spinach, thawed
1 Tbs. lemon juice
1 tsp. rosemary
1 tsp. thyme
3 cloves garlic, crushed
2 cups plum tomatoes, chopped
8 oz. goat or feta cheese
2 cups bread crumbs
2 Tbs. olive oil

Generously cover beans in sauce pot with fresh cold water. Bring to a boil, add bay leaf and reduce to simmer. Cook 30 minutes. Add salt and continue cooking 30-45 minutes until nice and soft, but still holding shape. Take out and save 1 cup of bean water, and drain the rest.

While beans are cooking, heat 2 Tbs. olive oil in large skillet, add leeks, saute until tender, add artichokes, spinach, lemon juice, and herbs, saute until heated through, about 5 minutes. Remove from heat.

Place beans, vegetable mixture, tomatoes and cheese in mixing bowl, combine gently to mix well. Pour into greased 9x13" baking pan. Add the cup of bean liquid. *(If you forget to save it, add tap water with 2 Tbs. white wine.)* Toss bread crumbs with olive oil to moisten. Spread evenly over bean mixture covering completely. Bake in 375 degree oven until beans are hot and top is golden, about 30 minutes. Let stand 10 minutes before serving.

Pasta Putanesca

Serves 4-5

1 lb. cooked pasta
1 Tbs. olive oil
1 medium onion chopped
6 large ripe tomatoes, chopped *(use some yellow ones for color if you have them)*
1/4 cup white wine
2 cloves garlic, crushed
10 Greek olives, pitted and chopped
5 sundried tomatoes, julienned
3 Tbs. chopped fresh basil
2 Tbs. chopped fresh oregano
salt and pepper to taste
flat leaf parsley to garnish

Heat oil in large skillet or shallow saucepan. Add onion and saute until just soft. Add all remaining ingredients. Simmer over medium heat until tomatoes break down and sauce thickens to desired consistency, about 35 minutes.

Serve over cooked pasta with parsley and parmesan cheese.

I love the name of this dish and had no idea what I'd be eating if I ordered it. It turns out that in general, it means a wonderfully robust tomato sauce, traditionally with anchovies and capers. I've replaced the anchovies with sundried tomatoes and the capers with Greek olives. At the height of summer, with fresh tomatoes, this sauce can't be beat.

You can serve it vegetarian, or add pieces of grilled chicken or julienned Canadian bacon. Lots of grated parmesan cheese – yum!

When I first started making this dish, I was told by a wonderful customer, Christine, that I didn't love my eggplant enough when I made this dish. Well, she was right; at the time I thought I didn't like eggplant. So, I made friends with it and realized it was a wonderful, meaty vegetable. Then, one of my employees, Amy, told me that you could tell the difference between male and female eggplants by the bottom indentation – if there was one, then it was a female and if it was smooth on the bottom it was a male. The male, it turns out has fewer seeds and tends to be less bitter. (Please don't confuse this with the human male species.) So look for male egg-plant, small to medium in size that you can love and you too, will have a delicious meal.

Eggplant Parmesan

Serves 6-8

Hint, the leftovers of the casserole made a wonderful and very popular sandwich at the store. Toast 2 pieces of wheat bread, a bit of mayo and a piece of hot eggplant parmesan – heaven!!

Eggplant layer:

2 medium eggplant, peeled and sliced into 1/2" slices
4 eggs
8 Tbs. flour

Whisk eggs and flour together to form a smooth batter. Dip eggplant slices in batter, allowing excess to drip off. Fry in large skillet in olive oil until just browned on each side. Drain on paper towels.

Tomato sauce:

1 Tbs. olive oil
1 large onion, chopped
2 cloves garlic crushed
5 cups chopped drained, whole tomatoes + juice from cans added back in
1 1/2 tsp. basil
pinch sugar
1 tsp. salt or to taste
black pepper to taste

Heat oil in large skillet, add onion and garlic, saute until onion is soft, add remaining ingredients and simmer until thickened, about 30 minutes.

To assemble:

1 1/2 cups grated parmesan cheese
1/2 lb. mozzarella, cut into small cubes

Cover bottom of 11 x 20" baking pan with half of eggplant slices, cover with half of sauce, sprinkle half of each cheese over, repeat with remaining ingredients. Bake in 350 degree oven 35 minutes or until cheese is golden and bubbly.

Summer Vegetable Lasagna

This dish was created in August when it had been 100 degrees for five days in a row. I wanted something that didn't take any pre-cooking and I also wanted to use up some rapidly wilting fresh vegetables. It was a hit!

Serves 6-8

12-15 cooked lasagna noodles, rinsed in cold water to prevent sticking
2 28 oz. cans crushed tomatoes
3/4 cup half and half
1/2 cup chopped flat leaf parsley
2 bunches watercress, chopped
1/2 cup sliced green onions
rind and juice of one lemon
1 Tbs. sugar
salt and pepper to taste

1 lb. ricotta cheese mixed with 1/2 tsp. salt and dash of cayenne pepper
1 lb. sharp white cheddar cheese ,grated
2 cups corn kernels, pureed until smooth
4 cups assorted chopped fresh vegetables I used: zucchini, yellow squash, asparagus, roasted red pepper and fresh spinach leaves

To make sauce combine tomatoes, half and half, parsley, watercress, onions, lemon and sugar. Mix well and season with salt and pepper.

Place a bit of sauce in bottom of 9x13" pan. Cover with one layer of noodles, cover noodles with more sauce, spread half of ricotta cheese over sauce, then half of corn, then half of vegetables, cover with half of shredded cheese. Repeat layer, ending with noodles and sauce.

Bake in 350 degree oven for 1 hour or until hot and bubbly.

A guy named Jake made this sauce one day for me. Jake didn't stay with us too long, but this sauce has lingered in my memory.

Cheese Tortellini

with parsley and thyme sauce

Serves 4

2 Tbs. olive oil
5 green onions, sliced
2 cloves garlic, crushed
1 1/2 cups chopped tomatoes, canned or fresh
1/2 cup chopped parsley, flat leaf if available
2 tsp. dried thyme or 3 Tbs. chopped fresh
1/8 tsp. basil
1/3-1/2 cup cream
12 oz. cheese tortellini, cooked and drizzled with olive oil

Heat oil in large skillet, add green onions and garlic, and saute for 1 minute. Add tomatoes and herbs, simmer 15 minutes or until thickened. You can add a bit of water if sauce seems too thick. Stir in cream – just enough to turn sauce a dark pink. Add salt and pepper to taste, and simmer for 5 minutes.

Serve over hot pasta with parmesan cheese.

Acorn Squash

with tomato pesto, sauteed vegetables and melted cheese

This is a wonderful way to use autumn squash. If you have tomato pesto already in the fridge, this is a snap to make.

Serves 4

2 acorn squash cut in halves, seeds scraped out
$^1/_2$ cup tomato pesto *(see index for recipe)*
1 large onion, chopped
3 medium zucchini cut in half lengthwise and then half again and sliced into $^1/_2$" pieces
2 cups quartered mushrooms
1 tsp. thyme
salt and pepper to taste
1 cup grated mozzarella or jack cheese

Place acorn squash halves in baking dish, cut side down. Fill pan with 1" of water. Bake squash in 350 degree oven for 25-35 minutes or until soft and fork pierces squash easily. Remove from oven and drain water.

While squash is baking, heat olive oil in large skillet. Add onion and saute just until starting to get soft. Add zucchini and mushrooms, thyme, salt and pepper. Continue to saute until tender, but still crisp.

Turn squash cut side up and fill each one with equal amounts of pesto, then fill with sauteed vegetables, and cover with cheese. Return to oven and bake 7-10 minutes at 400 degrees until cheese is melted.

Serve with rice.

Chicken and Poultry

Chicken and Poultry

I love chicken and turkey! I know that sounds totally blasé but lets face it, it's pure naiveté and wonderful lack of a strong flavor allows us to manipulate it into almost anything we'd like it to be. It is still fairly inexpensive, especially if you take the bones off the breast yourself. And in general, it is the safest thing to serve at a dinner party if you are uncertain of your guests' preferences. So – let's make it taste exciting, give that poultry some pizzazz!!

Wine Grilled Chicken

with black bean salsa

Great simple meal on a summer evening.

Serves 4

Chicken:

2 lbs. boneless breast of chicken
1 cup red wine
$^1/_4$ cup peanut oil
3 cloves garlic, sliced thinly
$^1/_2$ cup fresh basil leaves, torn into pieces
1 Tbs. tamari or soy sauce

In large bowl, combine all ingredients except chicken, whisk to blend well. Add chicken and immerse each piece in marinade. Cover and allow to marinate 4 to 24 hours in refrigerator. Remove chicken from fridge half an hour before ready to grill to bring it to room temperature. Grill chicken over hot coals until just cooked, juices will run clear and meat will become firm to touch – about 8 minutes per side. Remove from grill to serve.

Black bean salsa:

1 can black beans, drained and rinsed
1 large ripe tomato, chopped
3 Tbs. diced cucumber
$^1/_2$ cup chopped fresh basil
$^1/_4$ cup chopped fresh parsley
$^1/_2$ tsp. allspice
2 Tbs. fresh lime juice
$^1/_2$ tsp. tabasco
salt and pepper to taste

Combine all ingredients in bowl and mix well.

Serve chicken hot from grill, or at room temperature with black bean salsa and a basmati rice or a brown rice salad *(see index for recipe)*.

In the week of Valentine's Day, we'd have a dinner party at the Production Line Cafe with linen, china, flowers and candlelight. It was great fun and I usually served lamb. But on Valentine's Day itself, we'd offer special dinners to go. Raspberry chicken became a tradition. The sauce is not too sweet and the raspberries make for a luscious experience, even if it is not Valentine's Day.

Raspberry puree is a wonderful thing to have on hand for lots of things, such as ice cream, or add some vinegar and oil for a salad dressing. It will last in the fridge in an air tight container for three weeks.

Raspberry Chicken

Serves 4

2 lbs. boneless chicken breast
1 cup of flour tossed with salt and pepper for dredging
2 Tbs. butter
1 bunch green onions, sliced
$1\frac{1}{2}$ tsp. dijon mustard
1 large clove garlic, crushed
$1\frac{1}{2}$ tsp. raspberry vinegar *(use red wine if you don't have raspberry on hand)*
$\frac{1}{4}$ cup sherry
2 cups chicken stock
$\frac{1}{2}$ cup raspberry puree *(recipe to follow)*
1 cup cream
1 pint fresh raspberries
1 Tbs. honey
dash cayenne pepper
salt and black pepper to taste

Melt butter in large skillet. Dredge chicken breasts in flour, shaking off excess. Saute in skillet until golden brown and just cooked through, about 6 minutes per side. Remove from pan and keep warm. In same skillet, over medium high heat, add vinegar, green onions, mustard and garlic, cook 1 minute, scraping up anything stuck to bottom of pan. Add sherry and cook, boiling until you have a thick sauce. Stir in chicken stock and raspberry puree. Cook at high simmer until reduced by half. Stir in cream and fresh raspberries, cayenne and honey. Continue to cook until desired sauce consistency. Salt and pepper to taste. If the raspberries have too much of a tang you can add a bit more honey.

Raspberry puree:

2 cups berries *(fresh or frozen)*
$\frac{1}{2}$ cup sugar
$\frac{1}{2}$ cup water
1 tsp. lemon juice

Bring raspberries, sugar and water to boil in medium sauce-pan. Immediately remove from heat into bowl of food processor. Puree until smooth, press puree through strainer into a bowl to remove seeds. Makes about 2 cups.

Quick Chicken and Sausage Cassoulet

Before putting this in the book, I had Frances test the recipe. She left me this great message that it had become a request for birthday dinners by her family and I decided it qualified!

Serves 6

1 lb. mild or hot Italian sausage out of casing
3/4 lb. boneless breast of chicken cut into 1" pieces
1-2 large leeks, white and pale green parts only, sliced
2 carrots, halved lengthwise and sliced
2 celery stalks, sliced
1 28 oz can crushed tomatoes
3/4 tsp. oregano
1/4 tsp. thyme
2 15 oz. cans white northern beans, drained
1 cup bread crumbs, mixed with
1 cup grated parmesan cheese
2 Tbs. unsalted butter

Heat large skillet, add sausage, breaking up with spoon into small pieces. When just turning brown, add chicken, cook until chicken is just white, and add leeks, carrots and celery. Saute until vegetables are tender and meat is cooked through. Remove from heat and stir in beans, tomatoes, oregano and thyme, salt and pepper to taste. Pour into greased 9x13" baking pan, cover with breadcrumb mixture and dot with butter. Bake at 350 degrees for 35-40 minutes until top is golden brown and beans are bubbly.

Sometimes I would make a dish and feel like I could challenge Wolfgang Puck. This dish is one of those and I've served it at many a dinner party. I hate to be a parmesan snob and I think you can often use a domestic brand of parmesan cheese, especially if you can't justify spending the money on Parmigano, Reggiano. But I have to admit that it does make a difference when you use it. The rich, full flavor is a must in this recipe to make it taste as good as it can. Besides, good quality parmesan cheese lasts for a long time in the fridge and you don't need as much in a recipe as you do the domestic stuff. It really is worth the money.

Sauteed Chicken Medallions

with sundried tomatoes and parmesan cheese

Serves 4-6

- 12 sundried tomatoes, soaked in warm water until softened
- 2 cloves garlic
- 3 Tbs. olive oil
- 1 Tbs. olive oil
- 1 1/2 lbs. boneless breast of chicken, cut into 1 1/2" cubes
- 15 white mushrooms, quartered
- 1 tsp. oregano
- 1/3 cup white wine
- 1 cup chicken stock
- 1/2 cup freshly grated good quality imported parmesan cheese
- 3 Tbs. cream
- salt and pepper to taste
- flat leaf parsley and more parmesan for garnish
- 1 lb bow tie pasta, cooked, drained and tossed in olive oil

Drain sundried tomatoes and puree with garlic and 3 Tbs. olive oil in food processor until you have a nice paste. Set aside.

Heat 1 Tbs. olive oil in heavy skillet. Add chicken pieces and saute for 1 minute. Add mushrooms and three-fourths of the tomato puree and the oregano to skillet. Continue to saute until chicken is cooked and mushrooms are crisp tender. Remove from skillet and keep warm. In same skillet, add wine and deglaze (cooking liquid and cleaning up skillet) scraping any brown bits. Allow wine to reduce to 2 Tbs. Add chicken stock and remaining tomato puree, continue to cook at low boil until thickened a bit. Stir in parmesan cheese and cream, salt and pepper to taste. Simmer, stirring another 3-4 minutes, stir in chicken and mushrooms and any accumulated liquid. Serve over bow tie pasta with parsley and cheese garnish.

Grilled Chicken

with roasted red pepper and saffron sauce

Serves 4-6

Chicken: 1 1/2 lbs. boneless breast of chicken, drizzled with olive oil, seasoned with salt and pepper and grilled over hot coals until nicely browned and cooked through, about 6-8 minutes per side. Chicken will feel firm to touch when done. Remove and keep warm.

Sauce:

2 Tbs. butter
2 large leeks, white and pale green part only, cut lengthwise and slice
2 roasted red peppers, julienned *(I always use jarred roasted red peppers, Pelaponnese makes an excellent product)*
2 cups chicken stock
1/2 tsp. saffron threads
2 Tbs. fresh basil, julienned
fresh cracked black pepper
1/8 tsp. crushed red pepper flakes
1/2 cup cream
salt and pepper to taste

Melt butter in medium skillet, add leeks and saute until they just start to soften. Add red peppers and saute until leeks are tender. Add chicken stock, saffron, basil, black pepper and crushed red pepper. Bring to a boil and reduce by one-third, add cream and cook to desired sauce consistency.
Salt to taste.

For Christmas one year Vidula gave me a box wrapped in gold paper. I opened it to find gold, Saffron that is, Bunches of it!. Well of course I used it in everything for a few days, much to Frances' dismay. Seems, she had a run in with saffron once, using way too much in a dish and sending her family repeatedly to the "loo" all evening. So after much ridiculous laughter we limited our intake and came up with this great sauce. I served it on the menu with the chicken julienned over potato pancakes (in sides and sauces section) with the sauce over all, giving it a beautiful color and a lovely presentation.

This idea came from seeing oranges and tomatoes stacked on my counter. The thought of those two colors with flecks of green inspired me. This dish is very low in fat and takes minutes to make.

Grilled Turkey Cutlets

with orange basil tomato sauce

Serves 4

Turkey:

1-1 1/2 lbs. turkey cutlets (look in the poultry section of your grocery store)
1/2 cup orange juice
1 Tbs. olive oil

Combine 1/2 cup orange juice and olive oil and marinate cutlets in this for one half hour at room temperature. Grill over hot coals, 2 minutes per side.

Sauce:

8 ripe roma tomatoes
grated rind of 1 orange
1/4 cup fresh orange juice
1/2 cup fresh basil chopped
1 large clove garlic, crushed
salt and pepper to taste

Puree tomatoes in food processor and pour into saucepan or deep skillet. Add rind and juice of orange, basil and garlic, salt and pepper to taste. Bring to simmer and cook 5 minutes to infuse flavors. Serve over warm turkey with pasta or rice.

Roasted Chicken

with olives and potatoes

A good homey dish with a Mediterranean flair.

Serves 8

8 bone in breasts of chicken skin on
2 cups Greek olives, pitted and chopped
1 roasted red pepper, diced
2 cloves garlic, crushed
1/2 cup chopped parsley
2 Tbs. olive oil
8 medium baking potatoes cut into 1 1/2 " pieces

Mix olives, peppers, garlic, parsley and olive oil together in small bowl.

Set 1/2 cup of the olive mixture aside for the potatoes. Divide remaining olive mixture equally among chicken breasts. Stuff most of it under the skin of the breasts and smear some on top of skin. Sprinkle with salt and pepper and drizzle with olive oil. Place breasts in large roasting pan.

Toss potatoes with reserved olive mixture, salt and pepper to taste and distribute around chicken breasts.

Roast all in 350 degree oven for 35-40 minutes or until chicken juices run clear and it is cooked through. If potatoes need more time, remove chicken to plate and continue cooking potatoes another 10 minutes or until tender when pierced with a fork.

I had a great conversation with a customer one day after they had tasted my pot pie. He said he was skeptical because all he could remember were the turkey pot pies his mom used to serve – Stuckeys 4 for $1.00, with all those peas! All he would eat was the crust. Well, I had the same exact memory and that is what I was trying to dispel when I created this perfect comfort food. It was second to none in its popularity at the store. We served individual pies but I've given you instructions for a casserole dish to feed 6, or you, for 3 nights in a row!!

Homemade Chicken Pot Pie

with biscuit crust

Serves 6

Chicken:

3 whole boneless breasts of chicken

Lay out in baking pan, drizzle with olive oil, salt and pepper and add 1/2 cup of white wine to pan if you have it. Bake in 350 degree oven for 20 minutes or until just cooked through.

Remove and when cool enough to handle, cut into bite size pieces.

Vegetables:

1 Tbs. olive oil	5 stalks celery, chopped
4 carrots, chopped	1 large onion, chopped

In a large skillet, heat oil and saute vegetables until tender, do not brown.

Sauce:

5 cups chicken stock	1/4 tsp. basil
1/2 cup cream	salt and pepper to taste
1 1/2 cups milk	tsp. lemon juice
1 tsp. rosemary	1 stick butter
1 tsp. thyme	1/2 cup flour

Combine stock, milk and cream in saucepan with herbs. Bring to boil. While waiting for boil, make roux *(melt butter in small skillet, whisk in flour and cook until bubbling, for 2 minutes).*

Remove from heat. When sauce comes to boil, whisk in roux and cook, stirring until thickened. Add lemon juice and season with salt and pepper.

This is a great biscuit recipe for everyday use. Just make them bigger and when baking, either have them touching on the pan for a soft crust or separate for a crisper crust. If you want more just double the recipe.

Biscuit:

2 1/2 cups all purpose flour
1 tsp. rapid rise yeast
1 1/2 Tbs. sugar
1 1/2 tsp. baking powder
1/2 tsp. baking soda
1/2 tsp. salt
1/2 cup vegetable shortening
1 cup buttermilk

Combine all dry ingredients, cut in shortening with a pastry blender or your fingertips until flour resembles course meal. Stir in buttermilk until just moistened. Knead on floured board for 30 seconds, just to gather dough together *(the key to good biscuits is not overhandling them)*. Touch them as little as possible once you add the liquid or they will be tough. With a rolling pin or your hands, gently press out dough to 1/2" thickness. Cut into small rounds with a 1 1/2" biscuit cutter.

Gather scraps together to cut more rounds, using all dough.

Assembly:

8 slices mild cheddar cheese

Grease 9x13" pan, place chicken and vegetables into pan and toss together. Pour enough sauce over this to cover. Spread cheese over sauce and arrange biscuits over cheese *(cheese is to prevent the biscuits from getting soggy)*. Bake in 400 degree oven for 15-18 minutes or until biscuits are done and toothpick inserted in center of one comes out clean.

I haven't done much in the area of Tex-Mex foods, but this is an exception and I think it is really good.

Tequila Chicken

Serves 4-5

3 Tbs. butter
2 medium onions cut in half and sliced thin
2 cloves garlic
4 large boneless chicken breast halves, julienned
1/3 cup tequila
1 cup chicken stock
3/4 cup julienned roasted red peppers
1/3 cup canned green chilies
1 tsp. chopped fresh jalapeno pepper
1/4 cup chopped fresh cilantro
juice of 1 lime
1/4 cup cream
salt and pepper to taste
1 lb. fettucine, cooked

Melt butter in large skillet, add onions and garlic and saute until onions start to soften. Add chicken and cook until it just turns white. Add tequila and bring to boil. Cook for 3 minutes. Add chicken stock, bring to boil, stir in red peppers, chilis, jalapeno, cilantro and salt and pepper. Continue to boil until thickened, stir in cream and lime juice. Cook another 5 minutes.

Serve over hot pasta.

Chicken and Mushroom Casserole

Mrs. Janet Hoffheimer, God love her, was a picky customer. When she had this and told me she wanted it again I knew I had a winner. It's quick, has great flavor and overall appeal.

Serves 4-5

1 Tbs. olive oil
1 Tbs. unsalted butter
4 whole boneless breasts of chicken, cut into halves
1 1/2 lbs. sliced mushrooms
1 bunch green onions, sliced
1 1/2 tsp. rosemary + extra for chicken
1 1/2 tsp. thyme + extra for chicken
2 Tbs. tomato paste
3 cups chicken stock
1/3 cup white wine
1 Tbs. flour mixed thoroughly with 1/2 cup cold water
salt and pepper to taste
1 recipe mashed potatoes *(see meatless entree section)*

Melt butter in large skillet, add oil. Sprinkle chicken with salt and pepper and heavily with rosemary and thyme and place in skillet. Brown for 2 minutes on each side. Remove from pan and place in greased baking dish.

In same skillet, add mushrooms, green onions and herbs *(you may need a little oil in pan if too dry)* and saute until mushrooms are tender and most of the liquid has cooked off. Add stock, white wine bring to boil and stir in tomato paste. Stir in flour and water mixture *(making sure you have no undissolved flour in water or you will get lumps)*. Simmer until thickened, about 6 minutes. Pour over chicken and bake uncovered at 350 degrees for 20-25 minutes or until chicken is cooked through.

Serve over mashed potatoes.

I put these on the menu a long time ago because I thought they would be fun and I loved the name. Well, you loved them too, and soon, once a month we were making hundreds of pot stickers – not so much fun. Well I've cut the recipe size so that it can be fun again. They make wonderful appetizers or a first course and are great to make with your company while you visit with one another.

Spinach and Turkey Potstickers

with soy dipping sauce

Makes 25-30 dumplings

4 oz. frozen leaf spinach, thawed and liquid squeezed out
1 clove garlic, crushed
1" piece of ginger, peeled and minced
3 green onions, chopped fine
3 Tbs. chopped fresh cilantro
$^1/_2$ lb. ground turkey
1 egg
1$^1/_2$ tsp. soy sauce
$^1/_2$ tsp. tabasco or chili oil
$^1/_4$ tsp. salt
1 tsp. dark sesame oil
$^1/_4$ cup grated carrot
1 package wonton wrappers

Mix all ingredients together (except wonton wrappers) until well blended.

To make pot stickers:

Lay out wrappers, 4 at a time until you get fast at it so they don't dry out. Place about 1$^1/_2$ tsp. of filling into center of each wrapper. Take a pastry brush, dip it in water and run it along the outer edges of each wrapper *(this will help the wrapper stick together)*. Fold the wrapper diagonally, corner to corner and crimp the dumpling together in 4-5 folds to completely seal. Place on tray and cover with cloth until you are finish making the rest.

When done forming the dumplings:

Heat 2 Tbs. of vegetable oil in a skillet that has a tight fitting lid. Place pot stickers in oil and cook without disturbing over med-high heat until bottoms are a nice dark brown and have stuck to bottom of pan. VERY CAREFULLY pour 1 cup of water or chicken stock into skillet IT WILL SPLATTER. Quickly cover skillet and turn heat to low. Cook for 7 minutes. Remove lid and spoon dumplings onto platter. If you do this in batches, wipe out skillet before beginning again.

Serve with dipping sauce as a first course or add rice and salad for a meal .

Dipping Sauce:

1/2 cup soy sauce
1/2 cup white wine
3/4" piece of ginger peeled and sliced thin
1 Tbs. dijon mustard
Stir all ingredients together.

I vaguely remember my mother who is a good cook, making a dish called Coq au Vin. Actually, what I remember is chicken in a lot of red wine and cooked so long that my uncle would suck the marrow out of the bones. These are good memories, so when someone asked me to make this dish I decided to try it. This is dedicated to Mrs. Elliot, who always seemed to miss the nights we'd have this on the menu.

Coq au Vin

Serves 6

3 lbs. chicken thighs, skin removed
4 slices bacon, cut into 1/4" dice
3 small onions cut into large chunks
2 Tbs. flour
2 cups dry red wine *(the better the wine, the better the dish)*
1 cup chicken stock
1 Tbs. tomato paste
1 bay leaf
1/2 tsp. basil
2 Tbs. butter
1 lb. mushrooms, quartered
salt and pepper to taste

Cook bacon in large skillet removing to paper towel when browned. Drain all fat from pan except a tablespoon and brown chicken pieces on all sides, takes about 8 minutes per batch. Remove chicken to large greased baking pan. Drain fat from skillet except 1 tbl. and add onions, cooking until golden brown. With a slotted spoon, spoon over chicken. Add mushrooms to skillet and saute until all liquid is absorbed and mushrooms are tender. Spoon them over chicken. In same skillet, melt butter and whisk in flour, cook, stirring constantly 2 minutes. Whisk in wine, stock, tomato paste, bay leaf and basil. Bring to boil, continue cooking until slightly thickened, about 8-10 minutes. Season with salt and pepper. Pour over chicken and vegetables and sprinkle with bacon pieces. Cover with foil and bake in 325 degree oven for 1 1/2 hours or until chicken is very tender and sauce is thickened.

We served this over rice or mashed potatoes.

Meats and Fishes

Meats and Fishes

As I said before, I can't say I'm a vegetarian, but I rarely cooked with meats before the restaurant, and then mostly poultry and a lot of fish. Now I can do a pretty decent pork loin, a mean roast top round for roast beef sandwiches and have had the opportunity to be introduced to some other wonderful lamb and beef dishes. I must give thanks to all the butchers for helping me understand all those cuts of meat and to my very capable *meat* cooks, Frances and earlier on, James. Their confidence and ability in an area I did not know allowed us to serve top rate steaks, shanks and stews.

My Meatloaf

4 Tbs. unsalted butter
2 medium onions, chopped
4 stalks celery, diced
1/2 lb. mushrooms, sliced
1 green pepper, diced
2 tsp. salt
1 1/2 tsp. pepper

Melt butter in skillet, add chopped vegetables and salt and pepper. Saute over medium heat until soft, don't allow to brown. Set aside to cool.

2 Tbs. mayonnaise
1 Tbs. tomato paste
3/4 cup ketchup
1 Tbs. worcestershire sauce
1/2 cup cream
1 cup bread crumbs
2 tsp. basil
2 tsp. oregano
1/2 cup parmesan cheese
2 lbs. ground beef
2 lbs. ground pork
4 slices bacon

Whisk all ingredients, except meat, together until well combined, stir in cooled vegetables. Break up meat and with your hands, combine it well with vegetable mixture. Don't over work the meat or it will be chewy in consistency.

Form into 2 loaves on baking trays. Top each loaf with 2 strips of bacon.

Bake in 400 degree oven for 15 minutes, reduce temperature to 350 degrees and bake 20 minutes or until cooked through.

Great with baby carrots and mashed potatoes.

Makes enough for meal servings for 4 people for dinner and sandwiches the next day.

So many happy faces when I told people we had meatloaf sandwiches as a special for lunch. So many happy people who had our meatloaf for dinner the night before. This is for all of you. I miss making it for you. I think I miss the way it smelled in the oven most of all.

As soon as we put this on the menu, it was a regular hit. For the meat, Frances used round steak, but then discovered the cut sirloin tip *and seemed to think it imparted even more flavor.*

Frances' Beef Stroganoff

Serves 4-5

1 Tbs. unsalted butter
$1\frac{1}{2}$ lbs. meat cut into $\frac{3}{4}$" cubes
1 medium onion sliced
4 cloves garlic, chopped
$\frac{1}{4}$ cup water
$\frac{1}{3}$ cup white wine
1 tsp. salt
$\frac{1}{8}$ tsp. marjoram
$\frac{1}{8}$ tsp. thyme
$\frac{1}{8}$ tsp. pepper
1 Tbs. flour mixed with $\frac{1}{4}$ cup cold water until flour completely dissolved
8 oz. mushrooms sliced thick
$\frac{1}{2}$ cup sour cream

In large heavy skillet, melt butter, add onions, then meat, saute so all sides of meat are browned. Add salt and pepper, marjoram and thyme, $\frac{1}{4}$ cup water and wine. Cover and cook over low heat $1\frac{1}{4}$ hours. Add mushrooms and cook covered 15 more minutes. Stir flour mixture into skillet and cook, stirring until thickened. Stir in sour cream.

Serve over wide noodles sprinkled with chopped parsley.

Grilled Meatloaves

with bleu cheese sauce

When temperatures got past 80 degrees, my oven-baked meatloaf was just too hearty to be a good hot weather meal suggestion. So, we came up with a meat loaf you could throw on the grill. This also worked with ground lamb and made a great middle eastern burger.

Makes approximately 6-8 loaves

1 medium onion, chopped small
3/4 cup chopped parsley
1/2 cup bread crumbs
2 eggs
1 tsp. basil
1 tsp. oregano
1/2 tsp. paprika
1 tsp. salt
1/2 tsp. black pepper
3 dashes tabasco
2 cloves garlic, crushed
4 oz. mushrooms, chopped
1 1/2 lbs. ground pork
1 1/2 lbs. ground beef

Toss all ingredients together in mixing bowl, except meats. Mix well. Break meat into bowl and mix completely with other ingredients. Don't over work. Shape into 6-8 oz. oblong loaves. Grill on hot coals with lid on 7 minutes per side for medium.

Bleu cheese sauce:

1 cup homemade ranch dressing (see index for recipe)
4 oz. crumbled bleu cheese

Mix together until creamy. Serve with hot grilled meat loaves.

Grilled lamb burgers with cucumber yogurt sauce:

For lamb burgers change pork and beef to ground lamb. Change parsley to cilantro and basil to cumin. Form into burger patties and grill on hot coals about 5 minutes per side for medium-well.

Serve in a pita pocket with cucumber yogurt sauce *(see index for recipe).*

Early on I had a customer tell me that she finally figured out how to keep her Beef Wellington from overcooking thanks to a popular caterer in town, Jeff Thomas. "He said to roast the tenderloin until just rare, then quickly put this in the refrigerator to prevent it from cooking any further. Then when it has cooled, spread it with your paté, wrap it and bake it, it will turn out medium rare every time." Well, Jeff – if that is what you said – you were right! This was the other special every year at Valentine's Day and it is a treat.

Individual Beef Wellingtons

with mushroom paté

Makes 6

$3^1/_2$ lb. beef tenderloin, whole
salt and pepper
thyme
olive oil
mushroom paté *(recipe follows)*
1 package frozen puff pastry sheets, sheets thawed
1 egg mixed with 2 Tbs. water

Sprinkle tenderloin liberally with pepper, thyme and salt to taste. Drizzle with olive oil and roast in 350 degree oven until meat thermometer reads 110 degrees. Remove from oven and place promptly in refrigerator to cool down completely.

Make mushroom paté:

2 lbs. mushrooms, sliced
1 bunch green onions
4 Tbs. butter
1 cup sherry
1 tsp. thyme
8 oz. cream cheese
salt and pepper to taste

Melt butter in large skillet, add green onions and mushrooms, saute over medium high heat until liquid from mushrooms releases and evaporates. Add sherry and thyme and cook again until all liquid is absorbed. Remove skillet from heat. Pour contents into bowl of food processor, add cream cheese and blend until smooth salt and pepper to taste.

Allow to cool .

Cut tenderloin into 6 equal filets, between 7-8 oz. each.

Unfold puff pastry sheets and cut each into 4 equal squares. You can use the 2 extra to decorate your wellingtons.

Roll each pastry square into a square 2" bigger in diameter than the size of each filet to be wrapped.

Smear 1/4 cup of paté over 1 cut side of each filet

Place paté side down in center of pastry square and fold edges in to seal completely. You can brush a bit of water on edges of pastry to help with holding together. Flip over and place each wrapped filet on baking sheet, sealed side down. Decorate each with remaining pastry. You can cut out leaves, or hearts or whatever. Brush each with egg wash to coat. Bake in 400 degree oven for 20 minutes or until pastry is puffed and golden brown.

This is not an original recipe, but got such a good response I had to include it. Dear Ruth always asked me for an extra pint of many of our sauces and this is the only one I couldn't oblige her with since it is really just a glaze. But, what a glaze it is and it is quick, too.

Balsamic Glazed Sirloin Steak

Serves 4

$1\frac{1}{2}$ lbs. boneless loin sirloin steak *(thanks to a wonderful butcher, I found this fabulous affordable cut of beef)*
4 tsp. sesame seeds
4 tsp. vegetable oil
4 cloves garlic, crushed
$\frac{1}{4}$ tsp. crushed red pepper flakes
6 Tbs. sherry
2 Tbs. soy sauce
4 tsp. balsamic vinegar
2 tsp. honey
2 Tbs. cold unsalted butter

Season steak with salt and pepper. Spread 2 tsp. sesame seeds on one side. Heat oil in heavy skillet until very hot. Oil will begin to smoke. Place steak in skillet sesame seed side down. Spread remaining 2 tsp. seeds on exposed side. Cook $1\frac{1}{2}$ minutes per side for medium rare. Remove from skillet and keep warm.

Pour off almost all fat from skillet. Add garlic and crushed red pepper flakes, stir for 10 seconds, add sherry, bring to boil and cook until almost all liquid is evaporated. Add soy, vinegar and honey. Bring to simmer, stirring. Add butter and stir over low heat until incorporated. Spoon glaze over steak.

Teriyaki Pork Chops

Too often, pork chops are cut too thin and end up too dry when cooked. They should be plump and juicy. So, when I started cooking, instead of buying those pre-cut chops in the grocery store, I bought boneless pork loin and cut them myself! It is actually cheaper and you can make them any size you want. Add a great marinade, hot coals and some sangria and I'm happy!

Serves 4-6

Marinade:

1 cup white wine
2 cups soy sauce or tamari
1/2 cup brown sugar
1 Tbs. honey
1/4 tsp. crushed red pepper flakes
2 cloves garlic, sliced
1 large onion, sliced
2 Tbs. peanut oil
fresh cracked black pepper

Combine all ingredients well.

Cut 2 lbs. whole center cut boneless pork loin into 3/4" slices. Place them in a shallow bowl and pour marinade over. Let soak 2 to 24 hours covered in refrigerator. Remove one half hour before grilling .

Grill over hot coals about 4 minutes per side. Please do not overcook them or they will dry out. When they are done, they will feel firm to the touch and be just white all the way through.

I found a recipe similar to this a while back and put the dish on the monthly menu. When it came time to make it, the recipe was nowhere to be found. But the dish we made came out quite well and became a favorite. I recently found the original recipe stuck in some file. This one is much better!

Penne Pasta with Chorizo Sausage,

corn and roasted red pepper sauce

Serves 4-5

1 lb. cooked pasta *(we used the shape called penne)*
1 Tbs. olive oil
1 medium onion chopped
1 $^1/_2$ lbs. chorizo sausage, casing removed
$^1/_2$ cup roasted red peppers
2 ripe roma tomatoes
6 Tbs. olive oil
2 cups corn, fresh if possible, or frozen
salt and pepper to taste
parmesan cheese to garnish

Place peppers and tomatoes in food processor, puree. While machine is running, add 6 Tbs. olive oil. Mix until blended (about 15 seconds). Add salt and pepper to taste. Set aside.

Heat oil in large skillet, add onion and saute until just turning soft. Add sausage, breaking into small pieces with spoon as it cooks. When just browned on the outside, add corn and red pepper puree. Simmer 10 minutes to cook through. Serve over pasta. Garnish with parmesan cheese.

Lamb Casserole

with white beans and tomatoes

Nobody knew beans and meat better than James. This is a recipe he came up with and it soon became a classic.

Serves 6-8

1 cup flour
2 cloves garlic, crushed
1 Tbs. rosemary
1 Tbs. pepper
1 tsp. salt
2 Tbs. olive oil
2-3 lbs. leg of lamb meat, cut into 1" cubes
1 large onion, chopped
2 carrots, chopped
1 stalk celery, chopped
1 medium potato cut into 1/2" cubes
2 15 oz. cans white northern beans, drained
1 1/2 cups canned whole tomatoes, chopped
1 cup chicken stock
2 cups bread crumbs
2 Tbs. unsalted butter

Mix flour, garlic, rosemary, salt and pepper together. Toss lamb cubes in flour mixture to coat well. Spread out in greased 9x13" baking pan. Drizzle with olive oil. Bake, uncovered, in 350 degree oven for 20 minutes. Put browned meat in a casserole, add carrots, onions, celery, potatoes, and stock. Bake another 30 minutes covered. Stir in tomatoes and beans, salt and pepper. Top with bread crumbs and dot with butter. Bake uncovered for 35-40 minutes more until bubbly and golden brown and lamb is tender.

"What is a RAG-OUT?" was a very common question when this was the dinner item on the menu for the evening. Well, it is pronounced ragu, like the popular tomato sauce brand and is traditionally a stew with meat, vegetables, and tomatoes. This particular one is quite tasty with Moroccan flavors and simple to make.

Lamb Ragout

Serves 4-5

2 lbs. lamb, cut into 1" cubes *(leg of lamb or, thanks to Frances' husband Nick, we discovered a cheaper cut of lamb that works great in this stew – sirloin chops)*
1 $^1/_2$ tsp. olive oil
1 medium onion chopped
2 cloves garlic, crushed
1 15 oz. can whole tomatoes with juice, chopped
1 $^3/_4$ cups water
1 $^1/_2$ tsp. cumin
$^1/_2$ tsp. salt
$^1/_2$ tsp. sugar
$^1/_4$ tsp. pepper
$^1/_4$ tsp. cardamom
1 bay leaf
8 oz. baby carrots *(we used the ones ready to eat in a bag)*
1 20 oz. can chick peas drained and rinsed
2 medium zucchini, halved lengthwise and cut into 1" slices

In a heavy bottom saucepan with lid or dutch oven, heat the oil over high heat. Add lamb and brown on all sides. Remove from pan to a bowl. Reduce heat to medium, and add onions and garlic, saute 1 minute and return lamb to pot. Add tomatoes, $^1/_2$ cup water and herbs and spices. Bring to boil. Cover and reduce heat to easy simmer. Cook 45 minutes or until lamb is tender.

Stir in carrots, chick peas and zucchini, cook 10 more minutes until vegetables are tender.

Serve over rice or couscous.

Kyra's Crabcakes
with curry mayo

The first time I put these on the menu, I was a bit apprehensive. The recipe was from a place near the sea and crab was so expensive in Cincinnati. So, I adjusted the recipe a bit to make it affordable and these little cakes soon became second only to the chicken pot pie in popularity. The curry mayo really does them justice but you can use tartar sauce or lemon juice or anything else you like.

Makes 16 cakes

1 1/2 lbs. new red potatoes, boiled and mashed
1 red onion, chopped fine
4 stalks celery, chopped fine
2 Tbs. unsalted butter
1 lb. crabmeat
1/2 cup bread crumbs
1/4 cup chopped parsley
1 tsp. paprika
1 tsp. salt
1/2 tsp. pepper
2 tsp. tabasco
2 Tbs. mayo
2 Tbs. lemon juice
2 eggs lightly beaten

In medium skillet, melt butter and saute onions and celery until tender, don't brown. Set aside to cool.

Mix crabmeat, bread crumbs, parsley, salt, pepper, tabasco, mayo and lemon juice, stir in cooled vegetables, mix in eggs. Form into 16 patties and chill 1 hour. Heat 2 Tbs. vegetable oil in skillet. Pan fry crabcakes 3-4 minutes per side until nicely browned and cooked through. Let drain on paper towels.

Curry Mayo:

1 cup mayo mixed thoroughly with 1-2 Tbs. curry powder.

I will never forget Helen Hance's face when she told me how good she thought this dinner was. Her eyes half closed and she licked her lips.

Pan Roasted Salmon

with leeks and fresh corn

Serves 4

1 Tbs. olive oil
fresh cracked black pepper
1 1/2 lbs. fresh salmon cut into 4 fillets
2 Tbs. unsalted butter
2 leeks *(white and pale green part only, sliced)*
1 cup fresh corn kernels, or frozen
1 1/2 cups chicken or fish stock
3/4 tsp. thyme
1/2 tsp. paprika
dash tabasco
salt and pepper to taste

Heat oil in large skillet. Season salmon generously with pepper. Place skin side up in skillet and cook until color of fish has changed half way up the side, about 3 minutes. Flip and cook remaining side another 3-4 minutes until just done. Remove from skillet and keep warm.

Add 2 Tbs. butter to same skillet and melt. Add leeks, saute until just wilted about 4 minutes. Add corn stock and seasonings, simmer until just a tablespoon of liquid is left in pan. Serve over warm salmon.

Jumbo Shrimp Scampi
over linguine

Once in a while we all splurge – and this splurge is well worth it. Simple, earthy flavors, shrimp and garlic – what more could one want?

Serves 4

$1\frac{1}{4}$ lbs. large shrimp (15-20 ct.) or 5-6 per person
6 Tbs. olive oil
$\frac{1}{4}$ cup sliced green onions
5 cloves garlic, chopped
$\frac{1}{4}$ cup chopped parsley
$\frac{1}{4}$ cup chopped fresh basil
$\frac{1}{2}$ cup white wine
cracked black pepper and salt to taste
2 Tbs. unsalted butter
1 lb. linguine, cooked
parmesan cheese

In large skillet, heat olive oil, adding green onions and garlic. Sizzle for 30 seconds, add shrimp, toss in oil and saute 1 minute. Add parsley and basil, saute 1 more minute. Stir in wine and bring to boil. Simmer 3 minutes or until shrimp are cooked through. Remove from heat, stir in butter and salt and pepper to taste.

Serve over linguine with parmesan cheese.

Shrimp and Veggies

in hoisin sauce

Some time ago, I had bought this big can of hoisin sauce because I needed about a teaspoon for a recipe. There it sat in the fridge for months, everyone pulling it out thinking it was chocolate sauce. I had to keep telling them as their eyes watered and mouth curled, that it was an Asian condiment they were snacking on. Finally, Jody Veith called and asked me to make her a stir fry with shrimp for a party. I decided to be bold and to use some of that hoisin sauce. Good move on my part – Jody was pleased and we got a quick and delicious dish out of the deal.

P.S. You'll need hoisin sauce for my recipe for peanut dipping sauce and you can buy small jars.

Serves 4

1 Tbs. canola oil
1 Tbs. dark sesame oil
2 cloves garlic, crushed
1" piece ginger root, peeled and minced
6 cups julienned raw vegetables *(we used: carrots, zucchini, yellow squash, red cabbage – a must for great color, mushrooms, bell pepper – you can use these and more, whatever sounds good)*
1 1/2 lbs. medium shrimp shelled and deveined
1/3 cup hoisin sauce
2 Tbs. honey
1-2 Tbs. soy sauce or tamari
chili oil or tabasco to taste

Heat oils in large skillet over medium high heat. Add garlic and ginger and saute 1 minute until fragrant. Add vegetables and saute until just turning soft, about 5 minutes. Add shrimp and saute another 5 minutes until just cooked through. Add hoisin sauce, honey, soy and simmer another 5 minutes. Add tabasco to taste.

Serve over rice or pasta.

Grilled Salmon
with pineapple salsa

Living inland, I found that it was hard to get really good fresh fish unless you paid a bit of money for it. But I was always able to get great fresh Norwegian salmon at Biggs so that is what most of my recipes call for. You can always substitute another firm fish, tuna, swordfish etc. to your liking, especially with this salsa.

Serves 4

1 1/2 lbs. fresh salmon cut into 4 fillets
drizzle with olive oil and black pepper

Grill over hot coals, skin side up first, about 3 minutes per side, until just cooked through. Remove and keep warm.

Pineapple Salsa:

1 cup chopped fresh pineapple
1 roasted red pepper, diced
2 Tbs. diced fresh cucumber
1 Tbs. diced kiwi
1/2 tsp. allspice
1/2 tsp. cumin
1 Tbs. apple cider vinegar *(or other vinegar if you don't have this on hand)*
1 Tbs. olive oil
3 Tbs. chopped fresh cilantro
2 dashes tabasco
salt and pepper taste

Combine all ingredients and mix well.

Serve with grilled salmon.

You really get a lot for a little effort with this recipe. The sauce is quick and flavorful. It will make a lot, but I often got phone calls from people complaining they wanted more of that good sauce!

Shrimp with Spicy Black Bean Sauce

over linguine

Serves 6

2 lbs. medium shrimp, shelled and deveined
2 15 oz. cans black beans, undrained
1 Tbs. oregano
3/4 tsp. thyme
1 1/2 tsp. basil
1 tsp. cumin
1/4 tsp. cayenne
1/4 tsp. black pepper
1/2 tsp. paprika
2 Tbs. worcestershire sauce
3 ripe roma tomatoes
squeeze of fresh lemon juice, if you have it
2 tsp. salt
1 lb. linguine, cooked and tossed in olive oil

Combine all ingredients except shrimp in bowl of food processor. Process until smooth and adjust salt and pepper .

Pour sauce into large skillet and heat till bubbling. Add shrimp and saute until cooked through about 7 minutes.

Serve over linquine.

Sides and Sauces

Sides and Sauces

This section is a bit of a catch-all for all the smaller dishes and sauces we'd make to round out a menu. They are just as important and sometimes the key to putting everything together. Mix and match some main courses with some sides, and see what works for you. I love topping my potato pancakes with all kinds of things – grilled chicken, roasted vegetables, yogurt sauce, etc. Sometimes I'll wake up with a craving for something with sesame oil in it and build my whole menu around that flavor, starting with a noodle or salad dressing idea and going from there. Again, I've tried to give you some basic recipes that have a good foundation so that you can build something into exactly what you would like it to be.

Potato Pancakes

I absolutely adore potato pancakes – good ones – crispy on the outside, tender on the inside with a simple flavor and touch of onion. I was always intimidated to make them until necessity became the mother of invention. They really aren't that difficult and the touch of beer does the trick.

Makes 10-20 pancakes depending on size

2 eggs
$^1/_3$ cup beer
$^1/_2$ cup flour
1 tsp. salt
black pepper to taste
1 onion, cut in half and sliced thin
1 $^1/_4$ lbs. baking potatoes
vegetable oil for frying

Whisk together eggs, beer, flour, salt, pepper and onion. Shred potatoes into bowl of cold water, enough to cover potatoes. Soak 2 minutes and drain. Add potatoes to egg mixture and toss to coat.

Heat $^1/_2$" oil in frying pan. Spoon up a $^1/_4$ cup of potato mixture and place in hot oil, pressing down with spoon to form a patty. You can cook several at a time, but don't overcrowd the pan. Cook about 2-3 minutes per side until golden brown. Drain on paper towels.

Before I opened the store I worked as a private chef for a family for two weeks. It was their vacation idea for the year, stay home and act like you are in a neat hotel. So, the mistress of the house decided to have a cocktail party one evening and wanted to serve chicken satay on skewers. I had no idea what satay was, but before I could divulge my ignorance she produced a recipe she wanted me to follow. It seemed that satay was an Asian dish of marinated meats, skewered and grilled and then served with a peanut dipping sauce. She didn't let me keep the recipe and so I started on my quest for the perfect peanut sauce.

Satay

To make satay, we would marinate cubes of chicken, or pork in a simple mixture of half white wine and half soy sauce with slices of fresh garlic, ginger and crushed red pepper flakes. Let it marinate at least 2 hours and up to 24. Heat a grill and pierce the meat onto bamboo skewers. Grill over hot coals and serve with above peanut dipping sauce.

Peanut Sauce

Makes approximately 2 cups

$^{1}/_{2}$ cup chicken stock
$^{1}/_{2}$ cup creamy peanut butter
$^{1}/_{4}$ cup honey
$^{1}/_{4}$ cup hoisin sauce
$^{1}/_{4}$ cup chopped fresh cilantro
2 Tbs. soy sauce
1 tsp. dark sesame oil
$^{1}/_{2}$ tsp. crushed red pepper flakes
1 clove garlic, crushed

Combine all ingredients and mix well. Will store in an air-tight container in fridge up to 2 weeks.

I think I've tried at least 25 different versions of peanut sauce until I finally came up with one that I thought was really good. I originally found the recipe in a magazine as a marinade for pork and converted it to a dipping sauce for grilled meats, breads and vegetables.

Everybody wants casseroles around the holidays, especially intriguing vegetable casseroles that everyone will eat because they won't know there are vegetables in it. This is the best one we came up with.

Spinach Casserole

Serves 6-8 as a side dish

2 eggs beaten
6 Tbs. flour
16 oz. bag frozen leaf spinach, thawed but not drained of liquid
1½ cups cottage cheese
1½ cups grated cheddar cheese
2 cups fresh or frozen corn kernels
1 cup chopped sweet red bell pepper *(this is mostly for color and can be omitted if you don't have the pepper)*
½ tsp. salt
fresh cracked black pepper to taste

Beat eggs and flour in bowl until smooth. Stir in remaining ingredients. Spread into a 9" baking pan. Bake at 350 degrees for 1 hour.

Potato Salad

Makes about 2 quarts

10 new red potatoes cut into 1" cubes
$^{3}/_{4}$ cup mayo
$^{3}/_{4}$ cup sour cream
2 tsp. salt
$^{1}/_{4}$ tsp. black pepper
$^{1}/_{2}$ tsp. basil (1 Tsp)
$^{1}/_{2}$ tsp. granulated garlic

Cover potatoes in cold water in stock pot and bring to a boil. Simmer until potatoes are just tender when pierced with a knife. Don't overcook and make sure they are covered in water during the entire cooking time. Drain and cool.

Mix remaining ingredients together and add cooled potatoes. Toss to coat.

Lasts several days in refrig.

A– 7/19

Here it is, the potato salad recipe. So many of you have been kind enough to tell me how much you love it. I am happy to share it with you. A few hints for success: Use new red potatoes, leave skin on, cut the potatoes into cubes before you cook them, use Hellman's Mayonnaise and granulated garlic, or fresh, but not garlic powder. In the summer at home, I will often put in fresh basil or snipped chives instead of dry basil .

Cole Slaw

Makes 2 quarts

A lot of you love my cole slaw. I have to confess something – it's Marzetti Cole Slaw Dressing. There is nothing that compares in my book. We used 1 head of cabbage to 2 shredded carrots and enough dressing to give desired wetness.

My Rice

5 Tbs. butter or margarine
1 large onion, chopped
2 cups long grain white rice
4 cups chicken or beef stock

In medium saucepan with tight fitting lid, melt butter. Add rice and saute until beginning to turn a nice brown color. Add onions and continue to saute until rice is browned and onions are softened. Add stock and bring to boil, cover and reduce heat to low. Cook undisturbed for 15 minutes or until water is absorbed.

This is excellent with freshly grated parmesan cheese on it.

Actually this is my mother's rice recipe and when I was little I thought I would like to eat only this for the rest of my life. That was before I made my first chocolate cake!!

This was one of those other weird conceptions I had, that all salsa came from a jar, therefore I couldn't possible make my own. Well, I was way wrong and now making salsa is one of my favorite things to do. Once you have the basics down you can create, create, create!! Just remember, you need a fruit or vegetable as a base you would like to highlight. Then add your herbs, spices, flavor extras like chilies, onions, cucumbers whatever, some sort of vinegar and some sort of oil. Salt and pepper to taste.

Our House Salsa

2 cups chopped tomatoes *(fresh or canned)*
$^1/_2$ bunch fresh cilantro, chopped
$^1/_4$ cup canned green chiles
$^1/_3$ cup chopped onions
1 Tbs. cumin
1 Tbs. olive oil
2 Tbs. red wine vinegar
salt, pepper and tabasco to taste

Combine ingredients , mix well and let stand 1 hour for best flavor. Will store in refrigerator up to 10 days.

Roasted Red Pepper Salsa

(great on burgers!)

2-3 roasted red peppers
6-7 sundried tomatoes, soaked in water to soften and drained
2 cloves garlic
good size handful of flat leaf parsley, about $^1/_3$ cup
2 Tbs. olive oil
salt and pepper to taste

Combine all ingredients in food processor and puree until fairly smooth but still some chunks of peppers and tomato visible.

Fried Green Tomatoes
with peach salsa

We served this as a special lunch sandwich on wheat bread with feta cheese and sprouts on top. It was delicious.

Tomatoes:

3 unripe, green tomatoes, slice 1/4" thick
1 cup flour
1 cup cornmeal
1/2 tsp. salt or to taste
1/4 tsp. cayenne pepper
2 eggs beaten

Toss together flour, cornmeal and salt and cayenne. Dip tomato slices in egg, allowing excess to drip off and then dredge in flour mixture. Pan fry in hot skillet with vegetable oil until golden brown of both sides, about 2-3 minutes per side. Drain on paper towels.

Peach salsa:

2 peaches, pitted and chopped
1 roasted red pepper, chopped
1 Tbs. chopped fresh basil
3 Tbs. chopped onion
2 Tbs. chopped cucumber
2 Tbs. chopped fresh cilantro
1 tsp. lime juice
1 1/2 tsp. red wine vinegar
1 1/2 tsp. olive oil
1/4 tsp. cinnamon
3 dashes tabasco or to taste
salt and pepper to taste

Combine all ingredients, mix well serve with tomatoes. This is also great with grilled pork or fresh fish.

I'm sure I am partial, but I think that this is a great caesar dressing with no eggs!

Caesar Salad

dressing and croutons

1 can oil packed anchovies
$^{1}/_{4}$ cup fresh lemon juice
3 cloves garlic
1 Tbs. Dijon mustard
$^{3}/_{4}$-1 cup olive oil
fresh ground black pepper to taste

Place anchovies, lemon juice, garlic and mustard in bowl of food processor. Process until anchovies are pureed. With motor running, add oil in steady stream to give a nice creamy dressing. Start with $^{3}/_{4}$ of a cup and taste. If it is too tangy, add the remaining $^{1}/_{4}$ cup. Season with salt and pepper.

Croutons:

4 slices firm white, or wheat bread cut into $^{1}/_{2}$" cubes
$^{1}/_{2}$ tsp. oregano
$^{1}/_{2}$ tsp. basil
$^{1}/_{4}$ tsp. granulated garlic
1 Tbs. parmesan cheese
$^{1}/_{4}$ cup olive oil
salt and pepper to taste

Place bread in bowl and toss with oregano, basil, garlic and cheese, salt and pepper. Drizzle with the oil and toss again to moisten well.

Spread on a baking sheet and bake in 400 degree oven for 8-10 minutes or until golden brown and crisp. Allow to cool.

To make salad:

Wash and rip in pieces desired amount of romaine lettuce, toss with parmesan cheese and dressing and serve with croutons.

Green Bean Salad

Great on a picnic or a hot day when you've got a hankering for something green and cold.

1 lb. fresh green beans, washed and stems removed
1 tsp. lemon juice
1 tsp. olive oil
2 Tbs. olive oil
3 Tbs. red wine vinegar
2 cloves garlic, sliced thin
salt and pepper to taste

In saucepan, cover beans with cold water; add lemon juice, 1 tsp. oil and freshly cracked black pepper to taste. Bring to boil and simmer until tender about 15 minutes. Drain.

In mixing bowl, add beans, 2 Tbs. oil, vinegar, garlic and salt and pepper. Toss, cover and refrigerate 2 hours or up to 24.

The Best Mashed Sweet Potatoes

We used to have dinner parties at the restaurant once a month – a four course meal with china and silver. People brought their own wines and I went all out with fresh flowers and candlelight. They were great fun. The room filled with a different crowd each month and it really gave me a chance to be creative with menus. A standard fare in autumn was mashed sweet potatoes and I got a phone call from Beth, a regular dinner partier, to include them in my cookbook. I think the seasoning really high-lights the potatoes in this recipe.

10 smaller sweet potatoes, peeled and cut into chunks
$^{1}/_{4}$ tsp. nutmeg
1 tsp. sage
4 Tbs. unsalted butter
4 Tbs. milk or cream
salt and pepper to taste

Boil potatoes until mash tender. About 15-20 minutes. Drain and add nutmeg, sage, butter and milk or cream. Mash with hand masher until smooth. Add more milk if too stiff. Season with salt and pepper.

Mediterranean Eggplant Dip

(my version of baba ganouj)

2 medium eggplants, halved lengthwise
oil for brushing
4 cloves garlic
$^{1}/_{2}$ bunch parsley, flat leaf if available
3 Tbs. lemon juice
3 Tbs. olive oil
$^{1}/_{4}$ tsp. cayenne pepper
salt and pepper to taste

Brush cut side of eggplant with olive oil and place cut side down on grill over hot coals, or in preheated 400 degree oven on a baking sheet. Cook on grill 8-10 minutes or until nicely browned, flip and continue to grill until meat is tender. If baking, bake 20-25 minutes until easily pierced with fork and meat is tender. Remove and when cool enough to handle, scrape pulp from eggplants into bowl of food processor. Discard skin or if still intact, use as *bowl* for finished dip. Add remaining ingredients to eggplant and process until smooth. Adjust with salt and pepper.

Every time I read about this dish it seemed complicated – maybe it was the name. But one day, I found myself with a hot grill and some eggplants on hand. I took the leap and came up with this wonderful dip and soon the words baba ganouj were music to my ears!

For years I thought I should make my own ranch dressing, but it was so easy to buy it pre-made that I was never inspired. Then, one evening I found myself with a catered dinner going out that promised ranch dressing and I had none in the restaurant. So I made some. It tasted so good I never went back to the pre-made stuff!

Homemade Buttermilk Ranch Dressing

1 cup mayonnaise
1 cup buttermilk
1-2 large cloves garlic, crushed
1 tsp. basil
salt and pepper to taste

Whisk all ingredients together until smooth. This will gather flavor as it sits so try to make it at least an hour before you serve it. It will keep in the refrigerator for up to 2 weeks.

Artichoke Paté

2 15 oz. cans artichoke hearts in water, drained
3 cloves garlic
1/4 cup grated parmesan cheese
1/4 cup olive oil
1 tsp. fresh lemon juice
2 Tbs. tomato paste
salt and pepper to taste

Put all ingredients in food processor and puree until smooth.

One day a friend stopped by the restaurant with a small jar of artichoke paté he had bought at a gourmet store and a loaf of French bread. It was so good we ate the whole jar. I spent a year trying to find this stuff in every specialty food store I came across. It finally dawned on me that I could probably make it myself. It is great on pasta, pizza, breads, sandwiches or with a spoon!!

Great appetizers for all ages. Also great with hearty sandwiches like burgers and things.

Potato Fingers

with sour cream dipping sauce

Cut new red potatoes in half lengthwise, then cut each half into quarters, lengthwise. Place in bowl and drizzle with olive oil, sprinkle liberally with oregano, salt, parmesan cheese and black pepper.

Place in preheated 400 degree oven and roast for 30-35 minutes or until golden brown and soft inside when pierced with a knife.

You can change the seasonings to get different flavors, try rosemary, paprika, garlic, etc.

Sour cream dipping sauce:

1 cup mayo
1 cup sour cream
1 tsp. salt
1/4 tsp. black pepper
1/2 tsp. basil
1/4 tsp. granulated garlic

Mix all the ingredients together.

Makes 2 cups

Stuffed Mushrooms

These taste like little bites of Thanksgiving stuffing! They were requested quite often.

30 white mushrooms 1½-2" in diameter with stems
5 slices whole grain or firm white bread
2 tsp. sage
1 tsp thyme
¼ tsp. salt
black pepper to taste
4 Tbs. butter, melted

Remove stems from mushrooms and place the caps open side up, on a baking tray. Place stems, bread, sage, thyme salt and pepper in food processor and process until finely chopped, but not mushy. Place in bowl and stir in melted butter.

Stuff each mushroom cap with bread mixture. I like a lot of stuffing in each one and you should have enough to fill each mushroom ½" higher than the rim. Drizzle with olive oil and bake in 400 degree oven for 20 minutes or until golden and mushrooms are tender.

Serve hot or at room temperature.

These are so flavorful and make a really pretty presentation when sliced on a tray. You can serve them hot or at room temperature and the unsliced rolls will keep in the fridge for 1 week, making these great do ahead appetizers. This one is for you Gina!!

Sausage and Spinach Pinwheels

Makes 2 loaves about 14" long

1 recipe pizza dough *(see index for recipe)*
$1\frac{1}{2}$ pounds mild or hot Italian sausage *(remove from casing and cook, breaking up with spoon into small pieces, until nicely browned – drain off grease)*
16 oz. frozen leaf spinach, thawed and water squeezed out
1 cup grated parmesan cheese
olive oil for brushing

Cut prepared pizza dough into 2 pieces and roll out each piece into an 11x14" rectangle. Brush with olive oil, sprinkle half of cooked sausage over each rectangle. Then sprinkle on spinach and end with the parmesan cheese. Roll up jelly roll fashion starting at the wider side and crimp edges together to seal. Place on baking tray seam side down and brush with olive oil. Bake in 400 degree oven 30-35 minutes until nicely browned and roll sounds hollow when thumped. Allow to cool 20 minutes before cutting into slices about $\frac{1}{2}$" thick to reveal pinwheel design. Best if stored uncut and wrapped tight in refrigerator, or freezes well up to 6 months.

Pita Wheels

These were totally serendipitous and became the most requested appetizer for catered parties.

Makes 8 bite size wedges

1 loaf of Father Sam's Pita Bread *(a thicker, softer pita bread)*
$^{1}/_{4}$ cup tomato pesto *(see index for recipe)*
5 thin slices cucumber
3 slices jack cheese

Slice pita bread in half horizontally. Smear both sides with tomato pesto, cover one side with cucumber slices and then jack cheese, top with other side of pita, pesto side down. Bake in preheated 400 degree oven until cheese is melted, about 8-10 minutes. Allow to cool and cut into 8 wedges.

Vidula's Basil Sauce

straight from Italy

My assistant, Vidula, took, shall we say a sabbatical to tour the world for three months. She traveled to India, England, Ireland, France and Italy. I watched her go, very reluctantly, but anxious for reports on food, food, food. When she got back all she talked about was Italy and salami! She clearly had a love affair with this country and I finally got her to make this sauce. It is kind of a runny pesto with no nuts and tastes fabulous on sandwiches, especially salami!

2 cups packed fresh basil leaves
5 cloves garlic
1/4 cup fresh grated parmesan cheese
1 tsp. salt
cracked black pepper to taste

Combine all ingredients in food processor.

Process until smooth and with motor running, add 1 cup of olive oil. Process until thickened. This will be slightly runny.

Garden Brown Rice Salad

1½ cups brown rice
3 cups chicken stock

In medium saucepan, bring stock to boil, add rice and cover. Reduce heat to low and cook covered 45 minutes or until water is absorbed. Remove from pot, fluff with fork and allow to cool.

Meanwhile prepare the vegetables:

4 ears of corn kernels *(cook in boiling water for 3 minutes and then cover in cold water to stop cooking – drain)*
3-4 green onions, chopped
1 yellow bell pepper *(can be red)*, seeded and chopped
1 lb. fresh peas, shelled
2 ripe garden tomatoes, chopped
½ cup fresh basil leaves, chopped
¼ lb. fresh mozzarella *(I had this on hand, it can be optional)*
¼ cup olive oil
salt and pepper to taste

In a large bowl combine rice, vegetables, basil and mozzarella if using. Season with salt and pepper. Add olive oil and toss to coat. You just want a light coating, but add a bit more if this doesn't do it.

Let stand at least 1 hour at room temperature or up to 24 hours in refrigerator.

Every year I would close the restaurant for two weeks in the summer for a vacation and usually found myself in a lovely small town on the coast of Maine near my favorite Aunt and Uncle. My aunt is a good cook and one evening she invited us over for crab rolls and gave me the assignment of a side dish. Of course I wanted her approval but found myself in a small summer cabin with not many resources for elaborate cooking. This is the salad I brought and I was delighted when she asked me for the recipe.

This is an easy put together from recipes in this book and is definitely dedicated to the wonderful ladies at Blue Marble Book store in Oakley. It was a popular lunch special in warmer months and makes a healthy, filling meal with some pita bread.

Lentil Salad

Per individual salad:

1 cup cooked lentils
1 Tbs. finely chopped carrots
2 Tbs. crumbled feta cheese
2 Tbs. house vinaigrette *(see index for recipe)*

Place lentils on bed of hardy lettuce like romaine, sprinkle carrots on top and drizzle 1 Tbs. vinaigrette over, sprinkle feta on top of that and finish with remaining vinaigrette.

To cook lentils:

Lentils are quick to cook and do not require any soaking. Always cover lentils in pot with at least 3" of cold water and make sure they remain covered with water during entire cooking time. They take 30-45 minutes to be tender and still hold their form which is ideal for a salad.

Pasta Salad

Start with:

1 lb. box of pasta, cooked and rinsed in cold water to prevent sticking

Add to this, 3 cups chopped fresh vegetables, including some type of onion, red or green onion being the most popular. Season with a total of 1 Tbs. herbs and spices like dill, thyme, oregano, basil, cumin, paprika, cayenne, etc. We often added parmesan cheese, but you can change this to any kind of cheese, cubed or shredded. Salt and pepper to taste. Then add about $^1/_4$ cup vinegar and enough oil to coat well. If you want to make this a meal rather than a side dish, add grilled meats, ham, bacon or whatever.

1 lb. of pasta will usually feed 8-10 people as a side salad. If it is a meal, figure 5-6 people per lb.

How to cook pasta:

Always cook pasta in 4-6 quarts of water to 1 lb. of pasta. Season the water with 1 tsp. of salt for every 6 quarts. Bring the water to a complete boil and then add pasta, stirring until softened to prevent sticking. Cook at a boil between 8-11 minutes until just tender, but still a bit firm to the bite. Cook without a lid. Drain pasta. If eating immediately, add to sauce or coat with a bit of olive oil to prevent sticking. If holding and using later, rinse well with cold water to prevent sticking and further cooking.

Allan Smith sometimes ordered 2-3 catered luncheons a week. Each always consisted of a sandwich, pasta salad, cookie and beverage. We soon found out, thanks to Allan's candor, that we needed to be creative with these basics because he had to eat at every luncheon and would go crazy with the same thing over and over. I think we made 100 different pasta salads for that man!! Trying to be specific about how to make one seems a bit hard so I thought I'd share with you the same principles I'd give to my employees and let you too, be creative.

Desserts

Desserts

My favorite? We made so many things that I had a hard time picking the favorites. These were my stipulations: most often ordered as a whole cake or pie, and fastest to sell off the counter in pieces!

A lot of people think they can't bake, *"too precise for me"* or *"everything comes out dry or heavy"*. I am certainly not going to say baking a dessert from scratch is easy, but I do think a lot more people are capable of it. It really just takes practice! The employees who I allowed to bake for the counter, had little or no experience when they came to work for me. But after making a cake or cookies over and over again, they started to see great results. So, follow some basic tips below and chose a favorite or two and make it a few times. I think you will be pleased with your results by the third or fourth time. Then you can apply your experience to other recipes and mix and match ingredients and recipes and come up with desserts of your own! If a sauce or filling from one inspires you to combine it with a crust or cake from another – do it! Add fruit or caramel and you'll have something fabulous. You just need the basics.

Tips:

- When it says cream or beat sugar and butter until light and fluffy, that means light and fluffy, give it about 5 minutes. It will change to a lighter color and look lighter when it is ready. At the same time, don't over beat. Once you notice this change, unless specified, stop beating and go to the next step.
- In a world where we keep everything in a chilled space, it is hard to bake on the spur of the moment with room temperature ingredients. Although it is not a must, it will make a better cake if your butter is soft and the eggs and

liquid are at room temperature. This allows everything to blend better and a finer crumb will result.

- As a general rule, once you add flour to the batter, you don't want to beat it more than just to combine it well. The flour, if overmixed, seems to act like a lead weight, but if just mixed in until combined, the air in the batter stays put and you get a lighter cake.
- Don't over bake things! Bake it for the least suggested amount of time, even a bit less, and check it with a toothpick at intervals. The toothpick should come out clean in most cases or sometimes with moist crumbs clinging to it. Take the cake out of the oven as soon as you get this result or you will have a dry product. Wire racks help the cake to cool evenly and removing it from the pan while it is still warm usually prevents sticking if you have lightly greased and floured the pans to start.
- For best results I always use unsalted butter, no matter what the recipe calls for.
- People who enjoyed my chocolate desserts often commented that they weren't sickeningly sweet and I credit this to the chocolate I chose to use. Always semi-sweet, the darker the better – I never used milk chocolate. The brand we used was *Guittard,* not easy to find in the grocery store. Out of the choices available in most grocery stores, *Hershey's* is your best bet. I think *Ghiradelli* is way too sugary. Also, cool the melted chocolates to room temperature before adding them to the rest of the ingredients to prevent crusts from forming or a dry product.

Here's to great baking!!

I had the biggest compliment paid to me the other day. I was talking to a former customer and he said he missed my cookies. He compared it to when he was away at college and he'd wait anxiously for that Care Package from Mom with the coffee can of chocolate chip cookies. I thought that was a wonderful thing to say and did often feel like my customers' mother when they would come up to the counter and look at me with this cross of guilt and delight on their faces as they chose their cookie from the pile.

Chocolate Chip Cookies

Makes 24 4" cookies

2 sticks unsalted butter, softened *(I used a European butter called Plugra which is becoming available in specialty stores. There is less water in it and makes for a wonderful end result. If you use this butter, use 20% less than called for in this and any other recipe.)*
1 cup firmly packed brown sugar
3/4 cup white sugar
2 eggs
1/2 tsp. vanilla
2 cups unbleached flour
1 tsp. baking soda
1 tsp. salt
1 1/2 cups chocolate chips

In large mixing bowl, beat sugars and butter until light and creamy, about 5 minutes. *(Vidula beat hers 8-10 minutes and got a very large puffy cookie.)* Add eggs and vanilla, beat just until eggs are incorporated, about 1 minute. Combine flour, soda and salt, add to dough on low speed and beat on high about 5 seconds until just well combined. Stir in chocolate chips.

Drop spoonfuls about the size of a golf ball onto ungreased cookie trays. Bake at 325 degrees for 15-18 minutes until just browning for a chewy cookie, and until completely golden for a crisper cookie.

Cool on tray or racks.

These cookies have the best results out of a convection oven. You can use insulated baking sheets in a conventional oven for similar results.

Molasses Spice Cookies

with cream cheese frosting

A dear friend, Booney, who worked for me early on, brought us the recipe for the molasses cookies. They were delicious, but didn't sell as well as we'd hoped. Then another employee, Amy, came along and had the idea to top the cookies with our cream cheese frosting. A star was born!

Makes 24 cookies

$^{3}/_{4}$ cup sugar, plus additional for coating
1 $^{1}/_{2}$ sticks unsalted butter, softened
1 large egg
$^{1}/_{4}$ cup unsulphured molasses
2 cups all purpose flour
2 tsp. baking soda
$^{1}/_{2}$ tsp. salt
1 Tbs. allspice
1 tsp. cinnamon
1 tsp. black pepper

Beat sugar and butter until fluffy, about 3-4 minutes. Beat in egg and then molasses. Combine flour, soda, salt, and spices. Add to dough and mix until well combined.Form dough into golf size balls *(don't over handle or they will be tough)* and roll in sugar. Place 2 inches apart on ungreased cookie sheet. Bake at 350 degrees for 12-15 minutes or until just set. Cool. Spread top with cream cheese frosting.

Cream cheese frosting:

1 lb. cream cheese, softened
1 $^{1}/_{2}$ sticks unsalted butter, softened
4 cups confectioners sugar
1 tsp. vanilla
1 tsp. lemon juice, optional

Beat cream cheese and butter until light and fluffy, about 5-6 minutes. Add sugar one cup at a time beating to incorporate, add vanilla and lemon juice *(optional)* and beat until smooth.

Makes approximately 3$^{1}/_{2}$ cups. Will keep in fridge up to 3 weeks.

This recipe was given to me by a friend who got it from her grandmother, an old southern belle. I call it the cult cake. It started with Jeannie Messer and her clan. Then they told two friends and they told two friends and so on and so on. Five hundred caramel cakes later and I still don't know if the icing will come out right when I make it. But after a near fight in the dining room over who deserved to buy the last piece on the counter and countless whispers of "Oh gosh, she made it" as people walked in, it has been well worth the struggle.

Caramel Cake

Basic buttermilk cake layers:

Grease 3 9" cake pans and lightly dust with flour.

2 cups sugar
2 sticks unsalted butter, softened
4 eggs
1 tsp. vanilla
2 1/4 cups flour
1/2 tsp. baking soda
1/2 tsp. baking powder
1/4 tsp. salt
1 cup buttermilk

Beat butter and sugar together until light and fluffy, about 5 minutes. Beat in eggs one at a time, about 10 seconds between each, and add vanilla. Beat another 5-8 seconds until incorporated. Combine flour, soda, baking powder and salt, stir into batter alternately with buttermilk, ending with flour mixture. Mix just until well combined. Pour into 3 pans and bake at 350 degrees for 18-25 minutes, until toothpick comes out clean from center. Cool on wire racks for 10 minutes and then remove from pans and cool completely.

Caramel icing:

2 sticks unsalted butter
3 1/2 cups sugar
1 cup milk
1/2 cup sugar
2 tsp. vinegar
1 tsp. baking soda

In medium heavy bottom sauce pan combine milk, butter and 3 1/2 cups sugar. Cook over medium heat, stirring constantly until boiling. Remove from heat. In small skillet, melt 1/2 cup sugar until smooth and auburn in color, the deeper the color the deeper the caramel. CAREFULLY pour burnt sugar into milk mixture – it will bubble up – and cook over medium heat, stirring constantly until it reaches a temperature of 230 degrees on candy thermometer. Remove from heat, add vinegar and soda. Let cool 15-20 minutes. Beat with electric beaters until spreading consistency. Quickly ice cake before it cools.

Pie Crust

It's really not hard people, just don't over process it.

Makes 2 crusts for 9-10" pie or tart

$2^1/_2$ cups flour
1 tsp. salt
1 Tbs. sugar
2 sticks cold butter cut into pieces
$^1/_3$ cup cold water

Place flour, salt and sugar in food processor, and process for 2 seconds to combine. Add butter and process just until evenly distributed throughout flour. With machine running, add water in steady stream and process just until beginning to come together, about 30 seconds.

Gather into ball, handling as little as possible. Cut ball in half and flatten slightly into disks. Wrap each in Saran Wrap and chill 30-60 minutes.

The real key to this pie is the apples. For best results buy them from an orchard or farmers market and stick to the tarter ones for pies. In June I use Lodi's for a wonderful tart pie. In the fall I used a mix of Winesap and Rome Beauty and sometimes, if available Ida Red. If you run across an old fashioned apple, Golden Grimes or Wolf Rivers, snatch them up. They make a wonderful pie.

Apple Pie

2 pie crusts *(see index for recipe)*
5-6 good sized apples, peeled cored and sliced
3/4 cup granulated sugar
1/4 cup firmly brown sugar
1-2 tsp. cinnamon
3 Tbs. flour
2 Tbs. butter

Roll out one pie crust to fit into a 9-10" pie pan. Make it about 1/4" thick. Roll it out big enough to hang over edge by 1". Toss apples with sugars, cinnamon and flour and pour into crust. Dot with butter. Roll out second crust to cover apples and hang over edges by 1". Trim edges to even them out and tuck them up into side of pie to seal. Crimp. Cut 8 slits in top of pie, randomly about 1/2" long to allow steam to escape.

You can use extra crust to make leaves or shapes to decorate top of pie if you are feeling Martha Stewart like.

Place on baking tray to catch drips and bake in 400 degree oven for 20 minutes, reduce temperature to 350 degrees and bake another 50-60 minutes or until crust is golden and pie juice is bubbling out of slits.

Allow to cool slightly before cutting.

You can use this as a guide to my peach pie as well. Change the fruit to 8-9 fresh peaches, pitted and sliced *(never peel them)* and change cinnamon to nutmeg.

Sour Cream Apple Pie

1 pie crust *(see index for recipe)*
5-6 good size apples, cored, peeled and sliced
$^{2}/_{3}$ cup sour cream
$^{1}/_{3}$ cup granulated sugar
3 Tbs. flour
1 egg
1 tsp. vanilla
6 Tbs. granulated sugar
6 Tbs. brown sugar
2 tsp. cinnamon
$^{1}/_{4}$ cup walnuts, chopped
2 Tbs. butter

Whisk sour cream, flour, vanilla, egg and $^{1}/_{3}$ cup sugar until smooth, add apples and toss to coat. Roll out pie crust to over hang 9-10" pie pan by 1". Fill with apple mixture and roll overhang up into decorative edge.

Combine remaining granulated sugar, brown sugar, cinnamon and walnuts, mix well. Sprinkle over top of pie to cover. Dot with butter.

Bake at 350 degrees for 1-1$^{1}/_{4}$ hours until bubbly and apples are tender.

At Thanksgiving, we would take pie orders for several traditional types. Of course pumpkin was the most popular, but this pie always came in second. It also flew out of the store when we made it for the dessert counter. It looks so warm and comforting and the sour cream gives it a nice creamy finish.

A wonderful woman with a passion for chocolate cake, came to the restaurant often. She was kind enough to share this recipe with me. We named it the HO HO cake because it reminded me of Hostess Ho-Ho's in presentation – not taste! It is a wonderful, tall chocolate cake with whipped cream between the layers and a thick chocolate icing. It quickly became a favorite.

Ho-Ho Cake

Cake:

1 cup unsweetened cocoa powder *(not Dutch process)*
2 cups boiling water
2 3/4 cups all purpose flour
2 tsp. baking soda
1/2 tsp. salt
1/2 tsp. baking powder
1 cup unsalted butter softened
2 1/2, cups granulated sugar
4 eggs
1 1/2 tsp. vanilla

Grease three 9" cake pans and dust lightly with flour.

In a small bowl, whisk cocoa and water until smooth. Set aside to cool completely. Combine flour, soda, salt, powder in small bowl. Beat butter, sugar, eggs and vanilla until light and fluffy approximately 5-6 minutes.

On low speed, add flour mixture and chocolate mixture to batter alternately, ending with flour. Beat until just completely combined.

Pour into pans and bake in 350 degree oven for 25-30 minutes until tooth pick inserted comes out clean. Remove from oven and cool 10 minutes on wire racks. Remove from pans and cool completely.

Filling:

1 cup heavy cream chilled
1/4 cup confectioners sugar
1 tsp. vanilla

Combine in bowl and beat with electric beaters or whisk until soft peaks are formed. Keep chilled until ready to use.

Frosting:

1 cup semi-sweet chocolate chips
1/2 cup light cream
1 cup uns butter
2 1/2 cups confectioners sugar

In a sauce pan melt chocolate, butter and cream together until just combined and smooth. Remove from heat. Beat in the confectioners sugar until smooth.

To assemble:

Place 1 cake layer on plate, spread with half of cream filling. Place 2nd cake layer on top and spread with remaining filling. Place 3rd layer on top and cover entire cake with frosting.

People would ask me to make a coconut cream pie for the store. Much to their dismay I would refuse – coconut never has been a favorite of mine. But I finally agreed to indulge them with a banana cream pie that many thought was the best ever.

The Best Ever Banana Cream Pie

Crust:

$1\frac{1}{2}$ cups ground ginger snap cookies
$\frac{1}{4}$ cup ground almonds
3 Tbs. brown sugar
4 Tbs. melted butter
$\frac{3}{4}$ cup chocolate chips

Combine cookie crumbs, almonds and sugar in bowl, toss with butter to moisten. Press into bottom and sides of 9-10" pie pan. Bake at 350 degrees 10 minutes or until golden. Remove and pour chocolate chips into crust. Allow to stand until softened, about 3 minutes, spread to cover crust. Let cool.

Filling:

2 cups milk
$\frac{3}{4}$ cup granulated sugar
3 Tbs. corn starch
$\frac{1}{4}$ tsp. salt
3 eggs yolks
2 Tbs. unsalted butter
1 tsp. vanilla
2-3 ripe bananas

In medium heavy bottom saucepan, stir together sugar, cornstarch and salt. Whisk in milk. Place pan over medium heat, stirring constantly, until mixture just begins to boil. Reduce heat and simmer 1 minute, still stirring. Remove from heat, whisk about a cup of hot milk into egg yolks and blend well. Slowly whisk egg mixture back into hot milk. Place pan back on heat and cook for 2 more minutes at a simmer, stirring constantly. Remove from heat stir in butter and vanilla.

Slice bananas into bottom of crust, covering bottom. Pour custard into crust and smooth top. Place plastic wrap directly onto custard to prevent skin from forming and let cool at room temperature for 1 hour. Place in fridge and chill for 2 more hours or overnight.

Serve with whipped cream topping:

1 cup heavy cream chilled
$^{1}/_{4}$ cup granulated sugar
1 tsp. vanilla

Combine ingredients and beat until soft peaks form.

Yellow Cake
with strawberries, peaches and cream cheese frosting

This wonderful cake is an example of what I mean when I say, mix and match and come up with your own great creations. The cake is the basic buttermilk cake layers (see index for recipe) – which I use for everything! Fresh strawberries and peaches cover the cream cheese frosting (see index for recipe).

Take first layer of cake and spread with frosting. Cover frosting with slices of strawberries, and/or peaches. Top with next layer and repeat, top with last layer and ice entire cake with cream cheese frosting. One batch of frosting makes just enough to do the whole cake. When strawberries and peaches are not in season, try others – raspberries, blackberries, bananas, etc.

Cranberry Cake with Caramel Sauce

1 10" cake pan or springform pan greased and dusted with flour

2 cups flour
1 1/2 cups granulated sugar
2 tsp. baking powder
1/4 tsp. salt
3 Tbs. butter

1 12 oz. bag cranberries *(picked over to remove soft ones and berries cut in half to release full flavor)*
1 cup milk

With a spoon, mix together flour, sugar, baking powder and salt. Cut in butter with pastry blender or with your fingertips until butter resembles small peas. Stir in cranberries and milk until completely moist. Spoon into prepared pan and bake in 350 degree oven 30-35 minutes or until toothpick inserted in center comes out clean. Let rest 10 minutes and remove from pan to cool completely.

Caramel sauce:

I would wait until I was ready to serve this cake to make the sauce. You can even leave all the ingredients ready in the pan while you serve dinner and then heat it when you're ready for dessert.

1/2 cup granulated sugar
1/2 cup firmly packed brown sugar
1/2 cup cream
2 Tbs. butter

Place all ingredients in medium skillet and bring to boil, whisk constantly for 2 minutes until sugars are dissolved and sauce thickens. Pour over cake.

Cranberries – what a beautiful berry, like little jewels. This cake is old fashioned, simple and festive. And when you pour that caramel sauce over it, everyone will love you.

This brownie is the first one I made for the store. It has a thick chocolate icing and, depending on how long you bake them, they can be chewy and fudgey or cake like. We used to joke about drawing dollar signs in the icing on top of each one because they flew off the counter so fast.

Old Fashioned Brownies

Brownie:

2 sticks unsalted butter
6 oz. unsweetened chocolate
5 eggs
2 1/4 cups sugar
2 tsp. vanilla
1 1/2 cups sifted flour
2 tsp. baking powder
1 tsp. salt
9x13" greased baking pan

In medium saucepan over low heat, melt the chocolate and butter together, stirring until smooth. Remove from heat, allow to cool to room temperature. (*To melt chocolate: Heat the chocolate just until it is soft enough to stir it to smoothness. If you overheat the chocolate it will burn and become congealed and impossible to work with.*)

In a large bowl whisk together the egg, sugar and vanilla. In a small bowl combine the flour, baking powder and salt.

When chocolate is cooled, whisk it into egg mixture until well blended. Stir in flour mixture just until blended. Pour into pan. Bake at 350 degrees 30-35 minutes or until moist crumbs cling to toothpick inserted in center. A longer time will present a cakier brownie and less time a gooier one.

Icing:

1 stick unsalted butter
2 oz. unsweetened chocolate
1/4 cup unsweetened cocoa powder
1 tsp. vanilla
4 Tbs. milk
2 cups confectioners sugar

In a small saucepan melt butter and unsweetened chocolate until smooth. Remove from heat and whisk in cocoa powder, vanilla and 2 Tbs. milk until smooth. Whisk in sugar and remaining 2 Tbs. milk until smooth and spreadable.

Ice cool brownies. Can be cut into 12, 16, 24, 32 or 48 for bite size treats.

Pear and Cranberry Tart

1 pie crust
3-4 ripe pears, cored and sliced *(I like the brown skinned ones the best)*
6 oz. cranberries, picked over and cut in halves
3/4 cup granulated sugar
1/3 cup firmly packed brown sugar
2 tsp. cinnamon
3 Tbs. flour
2 Tbs. unsalted butter

Roll out crust to fit 10-11" tart pan, trim edges.

Toss pears and cranberries gently with sugars, cinnamon and flour. Pour into crust and dot with butter.

Bake in 350 degree oven 35-45 minutes until bubbly and fruit is tender.

I think pears are the most sophisticated fruit out there. Pictures of them look great on stationery. They sound elegant on a menu and have a fabulous taste. Alas, for the longest time I couldn't get my customers to eat them – until this tart. Maybe the cranberries diverted your attention from the pears or maybe the brown sugar made you think they were apples – I'll never know, but this tart is worth the attention it got. It is really simple and makes an elegant presentation.

This is my favorite dessert of all times and I don't even like peanut butter. I thought maybe I was partial to it because I had created it to fill that cream pie void in me. Then someone ordered five of these pies for her wedding and I decided it wasn't just me!

Peanut Butter Chocolate Cream Pie

Crust:

1 1/2 cups ground graham crackers
1/4 cup granulated sugar
1/2 cup semi-sweet chocolate chips
4 Tbs. melted butter

Combine graham crackers, sugar and chocolate chips. Toss with butter until moist. Press into 9-10" pie pan. Bake in 350 degree oven 10 minutes or until golden. Remove from oven and allow to cool.

Filling:

1 cup chocolate chips, placed in medium bowl
2/3 cup creamy peanut butter, set aside
3 cups half and half
4 egg yolks
2/3 cup granulated sugar
3 1/2 Tbs. cornstarch
2 Tbs. butter
2 tsp. vanilla

In a medium size heavy bottom saucepan, whisk together sugar and cornstarch, whisk in half and half. Place pan over medium high heat and when just beginning to boil, reduce heat and simmer, stirring for 2 minutes. Remove from heat and whisk some hot liquid into egg yolks, blend and whisk this mixture back into hot milk. Place back on heat and continue cooking at simmer, stirring for another 2 minutes.

Remove from heat, stir in butter and vanilla.

Whisk half of custard into chocolate chips until smooth

Whisk peanut butter into remaining custard until smooth.

Pour chocolate custard into pie shell, and gently pour peanut butter custard onto chocolate custard. Smooth top. Place plastic wrap directly onto custard and cool at room temperature 1 hour. Chill in refrigerator for 2 hours or up to 24. Serve with whipped cream topping *(see index for recipe).*

Raspberry Macadamia Nut Squares

This is a wonderful bar cookie with a butter crust and a raspberry, cream cheese filling, studded with macadamia nuts. I use to love to come in the restaurant in the morning and find one left over from the day before – a decadent breakfast treat! They make great bite-size desserts for a cookie tray.

Lightly greased 9x13" pan

12 oz. seedless raspberry jam
12 oz. cream cheese
$^{1}/_{3}$ cup whipping cream
1 cup macadamia nuts, roughly chopped, or you can use almonds
1 tsp. vanilla
2 sticks unsalted butter, softened
1$^{1}/_{2}$ cups granulated sugar
1 egg
3 cups unbleached flour
1 tsp. baking powder
$^{1}/_{4}$ tsp. salt

Combine jam, cream cheese and cream in saucepan and tirring over low heat, melt until smooth. Remove from heat and stir in nuts and vanilla.

In separate bowl, beat sugar and butter until light and fluffy, about 5 minutes. Add egg and beat to incorporate. Combine flour, baking powder and salt, add to butter mixture, and blend well.

Press half of butter mixture onto bottom of greased pan. Spread with raspberry mixture, crumble remaining butter dough onto top of raspberry mixture.

Bake in 375 degree oven for 40 minutes or until golden brown. Let cool and cut into 16, 24 or 48 bars.

Pecan Shortbread with Chocolate

This recipe has to be dedicated to David Parker. As soon as I put a plate of these on the counter, he would buy them all. They were a favorite of many others too, some people coming in just to see if I had made them.

1 1/2 cups all purpose flour
1/2 cup granulated sugar
1/2 cup pecans
11 Tbs. unsalted butter, softened
1/2 cup semi sweet chocolate chips
1 tsp. vegetable shortening

Combine flour, sugar and pecans in bowl of food processor. Process 5 seconds or until nuts are finely chopped. Add butter, process until dough begins to hold together, about 15-20 seconds. Press into an ungreased 9" cake pan. Score into 8 wedges, being careful not to cut all the way through. Bake in 350 degree oven for 30 minutes or until top is light brown. Remove from oven and cool. To remove from pan, insert another 9" cake pan into the one with the shortbread and flip onto bottom of inserted pan. Slide onto plate and cut into wedges.

Melt chocolate and shortening, stirring until smooth. With fork, or spoon, swirl chocolate onto top of shortbread. Allow to sit until chocolate firms up.

Index

A

Acorn Squash with Tomato Pesto, Sauteed Vegetables 51
Apple Pie 120
Artichoke Paté 103

B

Balsamic Glazed Sirloin Steak 76
Banana Cream Pie 124
Basil Sauce 108
Basil, Tomato and Feta Cheese Quiche 39
Biscuits 63
Black Bean Lasagna 45
Black-Eyed Pea Soup with Kale and Fresh Corn 13
Brown Rice Salad 109
Brownies 128
Buttermilk Layer Cake 118
Buttermilk Ranch Dressing 102

C

Caesar Salad 98
Caramel Cake 118
Cassoulet, Chicken and Sausage 57
Cheese Ravioli with Shitake Mushrooms and Fresh Sage 38
Cheese Tortellini with Parsley and Thyme Sauce 50
Chicken and Mushroom Casserole 65
Chicken Medallions with Sundried Tomatoes 58
Chicken Noodle Soup 5
Chicken Pot Pie 62
Chicken Salad Sandwich 30
Chicken with Olives and Potatoes 61
Chicken with Roasted Red Peppers 59
Chocolate Chip Cookies 116
Cole Slaw 94
Coq au Vin 68
Corn Chowder 6
Crabcakes 81
Cranberry Cake with Caramel Sauce 127
Cream Cheese Frosting 117

Creamy Broccoli and Carrot Soup 16
Creamy Smoked Turkey and Wild Rice Soup 11
Crispy Oven Baked Fish Sandwich 26
Cucumber Yogurt Sauce 28

E

Egg Salad 31
Eggplant Parmesan 48

F

Falafel 28
Frances' Beef Stroganoff 72
Fried Green Tomatoes with Peach Salsa 97

G

Garlic, Roasted 40
Green Bean Salad 99
Grilled Meatloaves with Bleu Cheese Sauce 73

H

Ho-Ho Cake 122

I

Individual Beef Wellingtons with Mushroom Paté 74

L

Lamb Burgers 73
Lamb Casserole with White Beans and Tomatoes 79
Lamb Ragout 80
Lentil Salad 110
Kale with Sweet Red Peppers and Onions 44

M

Mashed Potato Leek Pie 37
Meatloaf 71
Mediterranean Eggplant Dip 101
Mediterranean Sandwich 29
Molasses Spice Cookies with Cream Cheese Frosting 117
Mushroom Barley Soup 17

P

Pan Roasted Salmon with Leeks and Fresh Corn 82
Pasta Putanesca 47
Pasta Salad 111
Peach Salsa 97
Peanut Butter Chocolate Cream Pie 130
Peanut Sauce 91
Pear and Cranberry Tart 129
Pecan Shortbread with Chocolate 133
Penne Pasta with Chorizo Sausage 78
Pie Crust 119
Pita Wheels 107
Pizza Dough 40
Pizza with Roasted Garlic, Spinach and Mushrooms 40
Polenta with Sauteed Spinach 42
Pork Loin, Roasted 23
Pork Loin Sandwich with Apples and Cheese 23
Potato Fingers with Sour Cream Dipping Sauce 104
Potato Garlic Soup 8
Potato Pancakes 89
Potato Salad 93
Potato Soup with Sage 9
Potstickers, Spinach and Turkey 66
Pumpkin, Leek and Sausage Soup 18

R

Raspberry Chicken 56
Raspberry Macadamia Nut Squares 132
Red Pepper Salsa 96
Reuben 25
Rice 95

S

Salami, Melted Mozzarella & Artichoke Sandwich 27
Salmon with Pineapple Salsa 85
Salsa 96
Satay 90
Sausage and Spinach Pinwheels 106
Shepherd's Pie 35
Shrimp and Veggies in Hoisin Sauce 84
Shrimp Scampi over Linguine 83

Shrimp with Spicy Black Bean Sauce over Linguine 86
Sour Cream Apple Pie 121
Southwest Style Vegetable Chowder 7
Soy Dipping Sauce 66
Spanakopita 36
Spicy Cauliflower Soup 10
Spinach Casserole 92
Split Pea with Smoked Turkey Soup 12
Stuffed Mushrooms 105
Summer Vegetable Lasagna 49
Sweet Potatoes, Mashed 100

T

Tequila Chicken 64
Teriyaki Pork Chops 77
Tuna Salad, Melt 22
Tomato Brown Rice Soup 15
Tomato Pesto 24
Tomato Sauce 42
Turkey Cutlets with Orange Basil Tomato Sauce 60

V

Veggie Burger 21
Veggie Sandwich 24

W

White Bean and Vegetable Soup 14
White Bean and Vegetable Gratin 46
Wine Grilled Chicken with Black Bean Salsa 55

Y

Yellow Cake with Strawberries and Peaches 126